D1391627

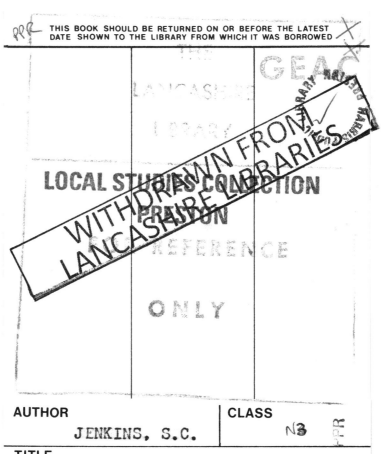

AUTHOR	CLASS
JENKINS, S.C.	N3

TITLE Railways across the Pennines

RAILWAYS PENNINES
across the

N

Haltwhistle

CARLISLE

NEWCASTLE

Alston

Workington

Cockermouth

Keswick

Penrith

Appleby

DARLINGTON

Tebay

Windermere

Dent

BARROW

Carnforth

PENNINE RLYS

OTHER LINES

ECML

MORECAMBE

LANCASTER

SETTLE

YORK

Clitheroe

Hellifield

SKIPTON

PRESTON

BLACKBURN

BURNLEY

Southport

BRADFORD

LEEDS

Todmorden

WIGAN

BOLTON

Rochdale

HUDDERSFIELD

Diggle

LIVERPOOL

MANCHESTER

Penistone

Hadfield

Hope

SHEFFIELD

Chinley

Dore

Lines described in text

CREWE

DERBY

RAILWAYS across the PENNINES

Stanley C. Jenkins and Howard Quayle

LONDON

IAN ALLAN LTD

Front cover, top:
'Black 5' No 45005 heads a summer Saturdays only Newcastle-Llandudno working on 9 July 1966. No 45005 is seen here climbing the 1 in 105 between Huddersfield and Standedge Tunnel near Milnes Bridge. *Gavin Morrison*

Front cover, bottom:
Class 37 Nos 37682 and 37677 head the 11.58 Peak Forest-Edale working on 14 April 1988. *Brian Denton*

First published 1990

ISBN 0 7110 1840 5

© Stanley C. Jenkins and Howard Quayle 1990

Published by Ian Allan Ltd, Shepperton, Surrey; and printed by Ian Allan Printing Ltd at their works at Coombelands in Runnymede, England

Half title:
Class 46 No 46026 *Leicestershire and Derbyshire Yeomanry* **emerges from Bowling Tunnel, and descends to Bradford with a summer Saturday Weymouth-Bradford working on 14 August 1982. Bowling Junction can be seen on the left.** *Les Nixon*

Previous page:
Electrics in Longdendale – Class 76s Nos 76031 and 76032 head MGR empties near Torside on the long ascent to Woodhead Tunnel on 9 September 1977. *Les Nixon*

Contents

PPR

Thanks are due to the staffs of both the University of Leicester Library and the Public Records Office, Kew, for providing research facilities.

To all the photographers who have provided material for this book, thanks are also due. Special thanks must be made to Tom Heavyside and Les Nixon, whose excellent work underlines their knowledge of, and love for, the Pennine landscape: to the late Derek Cross, a photographic legend, whose pictures of the long-vanished Stainmore and CKP routes have been invaluable; and to Messrs Lens of Sutton.

Last but not least, many thanks to Lynne Quayle for all the hours spent at the typewriter, and whose knowledge of Pennine railways must now be at least equal to that of the authors.

Introduction

Situated in the northwestern counties of England, the Pennines are a range of hills and moorland, running roughly from north to south and forming a formidable barrier between Lancashire and Yorkshire. These sombre uplands are not a homogeneous geological area, although as a general rule it could be said that the northern part of the Pennine Chain is formed of carboniferous limestone, whereas the southern fells are composed of millstone grit. In historical terms, the Pennines are remembered as the scene of the first Industrial Revolution, and Pennine towns such as Hebden Bridge or Colne remain as visible reminders of the days when over a million people toiled in the British textile industry.

In railway terms the Pennine region is of immense interest, not only because of the feats of civil engineering that were necessary when railways were built through this upland area, but also because of the relatively large number of pre-Grouping companies in the Northwest. The region was served by no less than 10 of the old companies, including the Great Western (which reached Lancashire over the metals of the Birkenhead Joint Railway) and the North British Railway (NBR) (which exercised running powers over part of the Newcastle & Carlisle line).

Each of these old companies was different, and even today the architecture of stations, signalboxes and bridges distinguishes each railway from its neighbours – thereby adding extra interest to even the most mundane of daily journeys. It follows from this that, although the omnipresent moorland (or mill town) scenery may impose an underlying unity on all trans-Pennine lines, each route retains a certain individuality and each has a unique history.

It is impossible, in a relatively small volume such as this, to deal with all lines within the Pennine region in great detail, but there is scope for detailed treatment of a selected group of lines, and this more circumscribed approach has been followed in the present work.

Chapter One deals with the Newcastle & Carlisle Railway (N&CR) which was the first trans-Pennine railway to be built. A significant section of this chapter covers the Alston branch in somewhat greater detail in order to show that not *all* Pennine routes were cross-country lines; this decision can be justified in that the branch concerned was an integral part of the Newcastle & Carlisle Railway (whereas other lines, such as the NBR route from Hexham were less intimately connected with the N&CR).

The next chapter covers just one line – the 'Little' North Western Railway (NWR) route from Leeds to Morecambe; like the Newcastle & Carlisle line this was an early trans-Pennine railway that followed a natural routeway from east to west. The Settle & Carlisle line, in contrast, was a much later conception, and one that did *not* follow any natural geographical route; there is, nevertheless, a logical progression from Chapter Two to Chapter Three because the lines concerned were interconnected and formed part of the Midland's drive to Scotland.

Chapter Four turns from the Midland to the North Eastern Railway (NER) line from Darlington to Penrith, and for completeness this chapter deals also with the Cockermouth Keswick & Penrith Railway – an independent line that formed a westwards continuation of the NER route from Darlington. Having examined the major routes north of Preston, the emphasis then shifts southwards to take in some of the former Lancashire & Yorkshire routes connecting Pennine towns such as Blackburn, Nelson and Burnley. (The lines described in Chapter Five connected with the Little NWR at Skipton and Hellifield, thereby forming a link with Chapters Two and Three).

Chapters six and seven examine the southern trans-Pennine lines between Manchester and Leeds, and Manchester and Sheffield; additionally, there is mention of certain connecting lines, including the recently-revived Copy Pit route from West Yorkshire to Preston via Rose Grove. Finally, the concluding chapter brings several disparate strands together, while attempting to foresee what the future might hold for surviving trans-Pennine lines. As well as discussing the role of Passenger Transport Executives (PTEs), the introduction of new Provincial Sector rolling stock, and changed operating methods, this final chapter also deals with the role of preservation societies and other matters relating to the Settle & Carlisle line.

Although it is hoped that the narrative will form a cohesive whole, each chapter can also be read on its own as a self-contained essay, and in this respect the various chapters are all different; some, for example, concentrate on historical aspects, while others place greater emphasis on architecture, operation or scenery. There is, however, a slight problem when dealing with lines that are still open; in such cases it is inappropriate to use the past tense when describing topographical details, and the present tense has therefore been used. Unfortunately, the pace of change is such that these details can become out of date almost overnight, and it is hoped that readers will appreciate that details relating to signalling, buildings, etc, were correct at the time of writing – but may, in some cases, have become dated as a result of continuing rationalisation of Victorian facilities.

CHAPTER ONE

The Northern Fells:
The Newcastle & Carlisle and Alston Routes

The Newcastle & Carlisle Railway

Running for over 60 miles through remote and beautiful moorland countryside, the Newcastle & Carlisle Railway was the first line to cross the Pennines — and also the first line to cross England from coast to coast. A very early railway, the Newcastle & Carlisle company was formed in 1825 and its capital of £300,000 was subscribed within the first few weeks.

The railway was built under powers obtained on 22 May 1829, and it was originally intended that the whole route would be worked by horses! As a result, when the first section was opened from Blaydon to Hexham on 19 March 1835 a local landowner objected to the use of new-fangled locomotives and was thereby successful in holding up services for several weeks. By 28 June 1836 however, the line was functioning as a steam-worked railway from Blaydon to Haydon Bridge, and on 18 June 1838 the

western end of the route was completed throughout to Carlisle; at the eastern end, the line finally reached Newcastle on 21 May 1839.

The early years of the Newcastle & Carlisle line contain several points of interest. Firstly, the company recruited in 1836 a 44-year-old booking clerk, Thomas Edmondson (who later worked for the Manchester & Leeds Railway) of Lancaster, who, dissatisfied with the time-consuming task of preparing stagecoach-type hand-written tickets, devised a system utilising small rectangular cards. The N&CR was not interested in this new system, and Edmondson was obliged to look elsewhere for backers. In a very short time, however, the Edmondson card ticket had become standard throughout Britain and most of the world, and although use of these traditional tickets had declined in recent years some BR stations retained stocks for day trips and other

Below:
The Newcastle & Carlisle line in 1990, showing pre-Grouping ownership.

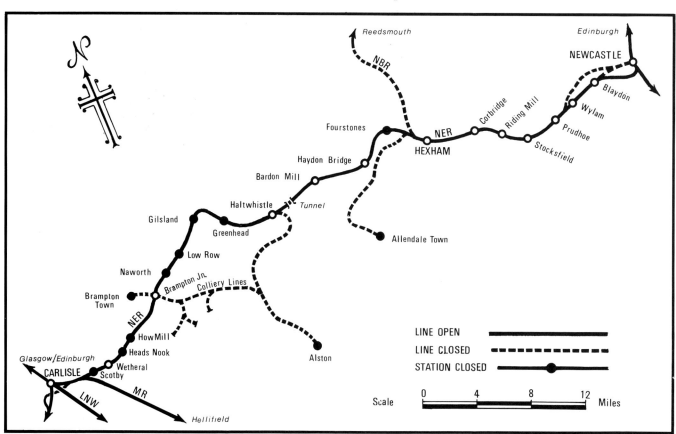

specialised bookings until 1989. A second notable feature of the N&CR was its use of right-hand running — a practice which continued for many years until 7 March 1864. Until the opening of the London & Birmingham Railway on 17 September 1838 the N&CR was Britain's longest railway.

The N&CR was the subject of much inter-company bickering, with the Caledonian Railway eager to take it over and the other West Coast interests determined that Newcastle & Carlisle trains should *not* use their joint station at Carlisle Citadel. Eventually, on 17 July 1862, an Act was passed to amalgamate the hitherto independent Newcastle & Carlisle company with the much larger North Eastern Railway — which had itself been formed in 1854 by the amalgamation of the Leeds Northern, York Newcastle & Berwick, and the York & North Midland railway companies.

The Route Described

In its period of independent operation the N&CR had used its own terminus in London Road, Carlisle, but following the end of the quarrel with the West Coast partners, Newcastle trains started to use the joint Lancaster & Carlisle-Caledonian Railway station at Carlisle Citadel. Leaving this ornate Gothic station, present-day trains strike eastwards across the flood plain of the River Eden, and rushing past the closed station at Scotby, soon reach Wetheral. Situated on a sharp curve amidst well-wooded surroundings, Wetheral is 4½ miles from Carlisle; the station was closed with effect from 2 January 1967, but was later reopened as an unstaffed halt on 5 October 1981.

From Wetheral, the double track railway continues eastwards, and travellers are rewarded with attractive views on either side as their trains cross the River Eden on a 95ft-high viaduct. Brampton, the next stop (11 miles) was the site of a junction with the Brampton Railway, a horse-worked line opened by the Earl of Carlisle in 1798. In later years, a horse-drawn dandy was provided to convey travellers to the main line station, and in 1837 the famous *Rocket* was purchased as a colliery locomotive; little now remains of this very early railway.

Continuing eastwards, the Newcastle & Carlisle line climbs high on to remote, windswept Northumberland moorlands then, crossing the Roman Wall in two places, trains descend towards the Tyne Valley. Haltwhistle (23 miles) was formerly the junction for branch services to Alston which ran southwards over a 13-mile long single

Top:
A four-wheel NER birdcage brake van stands on the Newcastle running line at Wylam during shunting long before the Grouping. *LPC*

Above:
During a period of main line diversions via Hexham because of engineering at Dunbar (22-24 July 1972) some of the N&CR passenger services were retimed. A Metro-Cammell DMU leaves Wylam bound for Newcastle and is passed by a Class 37 (No 6741, now 37520) on a pick-up goods to Hexham. *I. S. Carr*

Below:
Gradient Profile: Newcastle to Carlisle.
From Gradient Profiles NE13

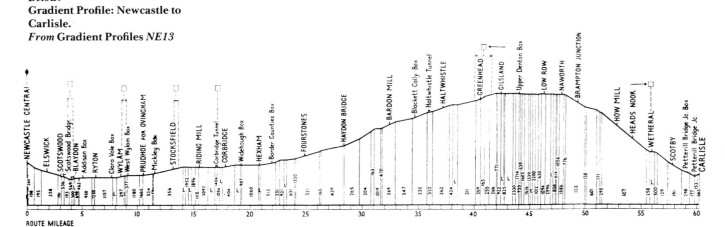

ROUTE MILEAGE

track line. Opened in 1852, the Alston branch was built to exploit local lead deposits, but sadly, this very scenic line was closed to all traffic in 1976.

Despite the loss of its junction facilities, Haltwhistle is still an interesting rural station. Staggered up and down platforms are provided — the eastbound (or Newcastle) platform being further east than its counterpart on the opposite side; the latter platform was once an island, with an outer face which served branch trains and allowed easy interchange for through travellers to Alston. Haltwhistle's up and down platforms are linked by an ornate footbridge, and the main station buildings are on the eastbound side. These buildings are (like those at many other NER stations) of Gothic design, and of considerable architectural merit; nearby, a solid, two-storey house provided suitable accommodation for the stationmaster and his family. Facilities on the westbound platform are more primitive, but the wooden waiting rooms, with their stylish half-hipped roof structure, are not without interest.

Other facilities at Haltwhistle have fallen victim to rationalisation, but in the pre-Beeching era the station boasted a substantial stone-built goods shed, extensive goods and marshalling sidings, and a small locomotive yard. A pleasing feature here were the wooden-post, ex-North Eastern semaphore signals which survived the 1923 Grouping (the home signal at the western end of the station was a particularly good example — it was *in situ* as late as the 1960s!).

Haltwhistle itself can be seen spreading out to the north of the station; a proud border town, it is less than two miles from Scotland, and the surrounding countryside is dotted with castles and peel towers which serve as poignant reminders of a turbulent and romantic past.

Leaving Haltwhistle the railway follows the West Tyne Valley, which provides a relatively easy path down to Newcastle — though the 19th century railway builders could not avoid a short tunnel between Haltwhistle and Bardon Mill (27¾ miles). Descending via Haydon Bridge (31¾ miles) trains pass two abandoned branch junctions; to the right, the NER Allendale line once trailed in from the southwest, while, a short distance beyond, the Border Counties Railway converged from the north.

Opened on 1 July 1862, the Border Counties line was a North British branch, penetrating some 30 miles into England! The NBR had running powers into Newcastle, and as a result, Reid 4-4-2Ts, 'Glen' 4-4-0s and other Scottish classes could often be seen around the eastern end of the Newcastle & Carlisle line. An early victim of rationalisation, the Border Counties branch lost its passenger services in October 1956 and was closed completely in September 1958 (apart from a short section between Bellingham and Reedsmouth Junction which lingered on until November 1963).

Hexham (39½ miles) was once the junction for Border Counties services, and is still the terminus of an intensive local service from Newcastle; the lengthy platforms here retain their glazed canopies and most of their buildings, which date back to the N&CR period. Perhaps the most

striking feature is the signal cabin, carried over the track at the eastern end of the station and affording the signalman a magnificent view of the line in both directions. South of the railway, the quaint old town of Hexham is well worth a visit, and travellers with time to spare should visit the remarkable Anglo-Saxon crypt of the Abbey Church.

Hugging the south bank of the Tyne, the railway continues towards its destination with an intermediate station at Corbridge (42½ miles). Pausing at other small stopping places the trains reach West Wylam Junction, where an alternative route to Newcastle formerly diverged to the left: this line was closed to passenger traffic in March 1968. Beyond the junction, trains run on a ledge above the river as far as Wylam (51¾ miles), the nearest station to George Stephenson's birthplace.

Until October 1982, eastbound trains crossed the Tyne after Blaydon (56¼ miles), and continued along the north bank for a further 2½ miles, passing Vickers engineering works before entering Newcastle Central station. To eliminate costly engineering works at Blaydon, however, the passenger service has now been re-routed along upgraded south bank freight lines, with trains joining the East Coast main line just west of King Edward Bridge. This re-routeing enables present-day Newcastle-Carlisle trains to enter Newcastle Central from either east or west, affording much greater operational flexibility during the morning and evening peak periods.

Although the Newcastle-Carlisle line fills a useful gap between the East and West Coast main lines, it was until recently worked as a self-contained line with a service of about 10 trains each way daily, and numerous shorter distance local workings between Sunderland and Hexham or Haltwhistle. Additionally, a small number of long distance cross-country services have been routed over the line in recent years. Until 1975, for example, Saturdays-only through trains from Stranraer to Newcastle and from Blackpool to Newcastle used the line, and in 1981, a daily

Carlisle-Newcastle-Edinburgh return working brought Class 55s and other large engines on to the route.

After a gap of some years as a self-contained route, the N&CR now once again sees wide-ranging workings, the summer 1989 timetable showing two Newcastle-Glasgow and two Newcastle-Girvan return workings, all handled by 'Super-Sprinters'. One of the Girvan trains is extended to and from Stranraer Harbour.

In addition to the sporadic appearance of diverted passenger trains, the Newcastle-Carlisle line is regularly traversed by heavy steel trains en route from the Northeast to a British Steel Corporation rolling mill at Workington; these air-braked company trains are usually double-headed by Class 37 Co-Cos.

The historic Newcastle-Carlisle line stills forms an important link in the BR network, but unfortunately the Alston branch is no longer with us. This route was nevertheless a great favourite among branch line enthusiasts, and it would therefore be appropriate to devote the second part of this chapter to a more detailed study of the Alston line.

The Alston Branch

Origins of the Line

Running southwards from Haltwhistle, and following the picturesque South Tyne Valley for some 13 miles, the single-track Alston route was built as a branch of the N&CR. The line was designed primarily as a means of tapping important mineral deposits in the Alston area, and its promoters clearly hoped that substantial coal and lead traffic could be developed once the branch was in operation. A modest passenger business was also envisaged, although the remote, underpopulated region through which the railway would run suggested that passenger traffic would always be subordinate to goods and minerals.

Left:
The 12.35 Carlisle-Newcastle, composed of two Class 101 DMUs and a trailing parcels van, passes the western portal of the abandoned tunnel at Corbridge, in the autumn of 1969. *K. Groundwater*

Above:
In the upper reaches of the Tyne Valley, a Newcastle-Carlisle working leaves Haydon Bridge station on 24 October 1981.
Tom Heavyside

A Bill was deposited in 1846, and despite sustained and sometimes bitter, opposition from local farmers and landowners, the scheme received its Royal Assent on 26 August. The resulting Act enabled 'The Newcastle-upon-Tyne & Carlisle Railway Company' to extend its existing line and make 'several branch railways', one of which would be the Alston line.

In common with other railway companies, the Newcastle & Carlisle suffered during the severe economic depression which hit Europe during the Hungry Forties, and the somewhat grandiose proposals foreseen in 1846 could not immediately be put into effect. Nevertheless, some work was underway by the early months of 1850, and at the half-year meeting held at Newcastle on 28 March the Newcastle & Carlisle shareholders learned that their directors were at last paying 'very serious attention to the Alston branch'. Construction was in progress, and negotiations had been opened with 'the proprietors of the land required'. It had in the meantime been necessary to amend the earlier Powers, and a further Act, dated 13 July 1849, permitted a series of deviations at Haltwhistle and elsewhere; a third Act was obtained on 29 July 1850 with the specific purpose of amending the existing Newcastle & Carlisle branch powers.

Work proceeded throughout the rest of 1850 and 1851; and having made considerable progress at the northern end, the directors decided that goods traffic could be introduced between Haltwhistle and Shaft Hill, a distance of 4¼ miles. The first trains apparently ran in March 1851; on 5 April *The Railway Times* reported that the branch was 'progressing', a portion from Haltwhistle to near Lambley being 'already in use for the conveyance of minerals and goods'.

Similar progress had been made at the southern end of the line, and although there was no immediate prospect of running through to the temporary railhead at Shaft Hill, the presence of a branch of the Brampton Railway at Midgeholme suggested that an alternative route might be created. Accordingly, in January 1852 mineral trains commenced running between Alston and the Brampton Railway; these workings made use of a special connecting line which diverged from the Alston branch at Lambley.

In March 1852 the N&CR directors reported that the line was 'open at both ends' and would be opened throughout 'on the completion of the viaduct over the Vale of the South Tyne at Lambley'. This impressive structure had nine main 66ft arches and seven 20ft spans; its height above water level was about 100ft, and the viaduct was approached by sharp curves on either side.

The Alston branch was finally opened throughout on 17 November 1852, but in common with many other lines, it seems that the route had been rushed into use before it was properly completed, and it is likely that local travellers were subjected to considerable inconvenience during the initial months of operation. Stations, for example, were probably still being painted and decorated, while ancillary items such as telegraph poles were not yet in place. Four months later, in March 1853, the Newcastle & Carlisle shareholders were informed that the branch was 'so far finished that it would come under the same arrangements as the main line from 1st April', but adverse weather conditions had impeded the installation of telegraph equipment and the necessary posts were not yet erected. On 1 April, however, the telegraph would be brought into use, and it was also announced that five stations on the branch and on the main line would be 'worked by clerks'.

The Line in Operation

The completed branch was soon carrying significant quantities of goods and mineral traffic, and there seemed every reason to agree with the directors' claim that the Alston branch would be 'greatly favourable to the parent line'. It would, they hoped, 'greatly increase the traffic and have a salutary effect upon their dividends . . . a great deal of traffic would be brought upon the line'. There was also talk of the distance from Alston to Newcastle being just 52 miles — the implications of this statement being that some through running may have been contemplated. In the event, passenger trains generally terminated at Haltwhistle, and NER timetables suggest that through running never became a feature of branch operation.

There were traditionally just three or four passenger trains each way between Alston and the junction; in November 1873, for instance, the branch train service consisted of three up and three down workings. The basic pattern of services had increased to four trains each way by 1900, and in June 1912 trains left Alston for Haltwhistle at 7.10am, 10.00am, 2.15pm and 6.30pm, returning from the junction at 8.20am, 11.50am, 4.15pm and 7.33pm respectively. An additional evening train ran on Saturdays, and the Sunday service provided two up and two down workings. A similar service was still in operation some 20 years later, and examination of the September 1925 LNER timetable shows that trains left Alston at 7.05am, 10.00am, 1.55pm and 6.55pm; the balancing down workings left Haltwhistle at 8.05am, 11.47am, 4.18pm and 8.00pm, but there was, by that time, no longer a Sunday service.

In addition to the regular branch passenger services, there were also several unadvertised workmen's trains between Alston and Haltwhistle — some of which called at a special colliery halt between Haltwhistle and Featherstone Park; known as Plenmeller Halt, this unadvertised halt was closed around 1930 after a life of only 10-12 years.

The timetable in operation on the eve of World War 2 was relatively complex by Alston branch standards, with six advertised trains each way daily. In the up direction, there were departures from Alston at 7.10am, 10.10am, 12.35pm, 3.55pm, 7.00pm and 8.20pm, with corresponding return trips from Haltwhistle at 8.10am, 11.30am, 1.35pm,

5.05pm, 6.20pm and 9.10pm. The 8.20pm from Alston was a through working to Carlisle, but curiously, public timetables did not show any down workings *from* Carlisle to Alston. Such workings were in fact provided — although they fulfilled no real public need and were a result of overall timetable planning rather than an overt desire to improve local train services.

Locomotive Details

In its earliest years, the Alston route was probably worked by former main line engines, but standard North Eastern classes such as the well known 'BTP' (Bogie Tank Passenger) class appeared in increasing numbers towards the end of the 19th century, and in the LNER period the branch was typically worked by 'G5' 0-4-4Ts, 'F8' 2-4-2Ts, 'J21' 0-6-0s and 'N8' 0-6-2Ts. Older types such as the 'BTP' 0-4-4Ts (LNER Class G6) still appeared, but the more modern 'G5s' had by that time become the 'classic' Alston branch locomotive type. The 'G5' 0-4-4Ts were destined to enjoy a particularly long association with the line, and one of these familiar ex-NER locomotives was usually sub-shedded at Alston; in BR days Nos 67315 and 62741 became regular performers.

Classes used on the branch in more recent years included (in addition to 'G5' 0-4-4Ts and 'J21' 0-6-0s), 'J39' 0-6-0s, ex-LMS Ivatt Class 4MT 2-6-0s, BR Standard Class 3MT 2-6-0s, and Standard Class 4MT 2-6-0s. Typical numbers, around 1950-58 included '3MT' No 77011 and 4MTs Nos 43126 and 43128, together with 'J39' 0-6-0s Nos 64812, 64814, 64842 and 64849.

Below:
On 6 October 1973, preserved 'A4' 4-6-2 No 4498 *Sir Nigel Gresley* passes the NER signalbox at Blenkinsop with the eastbound 'Tynesider'. *Tom Heavyside*

The Route Described

Alston branch trains departed from the southernmost of Haltwhistle's three platforms and ran eastwards for a short distance before diverging abruptly southeastwards on to the single track branch. Climbing slightly, the line curved southwards in a great arc which took it through a full 90° turn. Trains then crossed the sparkling South Tyne for the first time on a graceful arched viaduct – the first of many on this heavily-engineered scenic route. Having reached the south bank of the river, the railway soon entered a substantial cutting as it meandered on to a southwesterly heading for the first part of its run down the South Tyne Valley.

With patches of moorland visible on all sides, trains crossed a minor road on the level, and soon reached the first intermediate station at Featherstone Park, which was 3 miles 7 chains from Haltwhistle. Situated in a remote position, this small stopping place served the inhabitants of Rowfoot – a tiny hamlet to the east of the railway. Featherstone Castle was less than a mile to the west, and it is interesting to note that prisoners of war were kept here during World War 2. Beyond, the single line continued southwards, passing the remains of private sidings which once served nearby Featherstone colliery.

Coanwood, the next stop was 4 miles 18 chains from Haltwhistle and like Featherstone Park, it served a rural mining community of coal miners and quarrymen; Coanwood colliery was more or less adjacent to the station, while Coanwood Whinstone quarry was half a mile further on.

From Coanwood the route continued southwestwards, crossing the South Tyne Viaduct and immediately entering Lambley station. Situated on a sharp curve, Lambley was 4 miles 67 chains from Haltwhistle and boasted a range of attractive Jacobean-style station buildings with a prom-

inent central gable. Toilet and waiting room facilities were provided in a single-storey wooden extension to the south of the main building, and there was a small hip-roofed signalbox to the north. The view from the platform was most impressive, with Lambley Viaduct dominating the scene in the foreground, and the unspoiled river flowing and bubbling beneath. Northwards, the remains of the connecting line to Bampton could clearly be seen; this abandoned branch formerly served Lambley colliery and a variety of other mines and quarries en route to Brampton Junction and Brampton.

Apart from its coal and mineral traffic, Lambley also handled small amounts of other goods, including agricultural produce from the surrounding farms and general merchandise for consumption in the immediate locality. Passenger traffic was never heavy, but the station nevertheless served the needs of Lambley's few hundred inhabitants for many years. Amusingly, Henry Laing – the stationmaster here around 1890 – was also a sub-postmaster and Lambley station doubled as the village Post Office! (An unusual, but by no means unique, situation in remote moorland areas.)

Departing from Lambley, down trains followed the west bank of the South Tyne, with the B6277 running parallel to the right and high moorland visible on either side. The line climbed steeply, and there were numerous arched bridges and viaducts across fast-flowing moorland streams. Slaggyford, some 8 miles 49 chains from Haltwhistle, was particularly picturesque, with a screen of trees and shrubs providing at least some protection from winter wind and

On 14 November 1981, Class 47 No 47009 crosses the River Eden at Wetheral, just outside Carlisle, with the 09.40 from Edinburgh. With one stop, at Hexham, this train covered the 60¼ miles between Newcastle and Carlisle in 81min.
Tom Heavyside

rain. In its heyday, this station had boasted a passing loop, a signalbox, a local coal yard and loading bank and a private siding which served a limestone company; a minor road crossed the line on the level to the south of the platform.

Leaving Slaggyford trains resumed their ascent towards Alston, with the South Tyne still visible to the east and 2,000ft-high fells towering above the railway on its west side. Nearing their destination trains crossed the county boundary between Northumberland and Cumberland, then rumbled across the river for the third and last time, and with four long stone sidings running parallel to the left the 13-mile 14-chain journey from Haltwhistle came to an end.

The terminus was an interesting mid-Victorian station replete with a variety of unusual features. When first opened, the line had probably terminated beside a single platform, with a run-round loop to the west and a small turntable at the very end of the line; in later years, what had been the engine release road was apparently truncated to form a short, dead-end siding, and it seems likely that a new release road was installed to the west of the old one. There was a small, stone-built engine shed beside the passenger station, and this too was served by a direct connection to the turntable – enabling incoming locomotives to retire to the shed after uncoupling and drawing forward on to the turntable.

The main station buildings were on the down (ie east) side of the line, and were built in the Jacobean style with mullioned windows, tall chimneys and decorative gables.

The single platform was protected by an overall roof which rested upon a buttressed wall on one side, and the station building on the other. The engine shed, with its workshops and water tower, was joined to the train shed, and there was, as a result, an interesting range of architecturally-similar structures grouped together at the end of the line. All were built of semi-irregular stonework which was laid for the most part in horizontal courses with occasional patches of 'snecked' masonry; the main station building was, in later years at least, covered with cement (or similar) rendering on its three most exposed sides (one wonders if the stationmaster's accommodation was susceptible to damp?)

Alston's track plan was relatively complex, and in addition to its run-round and locomotive facilities this Pennine branch terminus had extensive goods sidings, with a hip-roofed goods shed and some characteristic NER coal drops; one of the yard sidings extended southwards and, passing beneath a road overbridge, terminated in a privately-owned stone yard. Other facilities included the usual loading docks, cattle pens, and a four-ton yard crane. There was no coaling stage and engines were hand-coaled from wagons standing on a specially provided spur beside the locomotive shed; water was obtained from an elegant swan-necked water crane of classic NER design.

Unusually the southern end of the passenger platform terminated in a flight of stone steps instead of the customary sloping ramp – which was in a sense illegal under normal Board of Trade regulations (although the fact that this end of the platform was not used by departing trains presumably meant that a conventional ramp was unnecessary). Another of Alston's unusual features were its interlaced turnouts or – to use their local name – 'sleepered leads'; such turnouts made use of ordinary sleepers in lieu of the extra-long timbers normally employed in pointwork, and they were at one time common throughout the former NER system.

The terminus was fully signalled, and, even in the postwar period, railway archaeologists could have found genuine ex-NER slotted post semaphores, complete with their stylish, McKenzie & Holland-pattern finials; the bracketed down home was a particularly long-lived example, though sadly this NER veteran had lost its distinctive 4ft high finial. The station was controlled from a brick-built signalbox standing on the up side of the line which had apparently replaced a timber-built original around 1900. The replacement box was a hip-roofed design which, in true North Eastern fashion, carried 'ALSTON' nameboards on each side rather than on the main facade.

In employment terms, Alston station was comparatively important, and in a small community its labour force of porters, booking clerks, permanent way men, labourers and locomotive crews constituted a sizeable chunk of the working population (there were generally four sets of locomen here at any one time). The stationmaster, in 1894, was Joseph Walton; later, around 1925, the local stationmaster was Joseph Little.

The Final Years

The Alston to Haltwhistle line was dieselised in 1959, and in the next few years Metro-Cammell two-car sets became familiar sights in the South Tyne Valley. In 1965 the usual vehicles were replaced by four-wheeled railbuses Nos E79963 and E79964, but these lightweight units could not haul parcels vans, and were difficult to heat during spells of cold weather; by 1966, both had been sent elsewhere.

The dieselised train service provide no more than six or seven workings each way. In May 1971, for instance, there were departures from Haltwhistle to Alston at 06.19, 08.19, 12 noon, 15.34, 17.42 and 20.30, while in the reverse direction the balancing up services left Alston at 06.58, 08.58, 12.55, 16.13, 18.50 and 21.09 respectively. An additional train ran on Saturdays, and this provided an extra round trip from Haltwhistle at 10.15, with a corresponding return journey from Alston at 10.53.

Unfortunately, the positive aspects of dieselisation were not exploited to their fullest potential, and whereas in Germany (or other advanced nations) modernisation was seen as a means of getting more people on to the railways, BR succeeded only in driving customers on to the roads in ever-increasing numbers. It is staggering, for example, to find that most forms of cheap day return tickets were abolished coincidentally with dieselisation, and for this reason fares doubled on the day that the new multiple-units entered regular service. Local travellers became convinced that their line was being run down prior to closure, and this belief was reinforced by the sight of boarded stations and acres of derelict sidings; by 1962 the line was said to be 'losing' £6,000 a year. Neither did the form taken by modernisation on the Alston branch lead to appreciable savings, and there was considerable wastage involved in regular empty stock workings to and from South Gosforth or Hexham sheds at the start and end of each day's service (one wonders, for example, why the branch set could not have been stationed at Haltwhistle, with consequent savings in terms of fuel consumption?). Perhaps the worst blow in the run-up to closure came in 1960 when the Anglo-Austral Mines of Nenthead decided to send their

Below:
A 1970s view of Coanwood on the Alston-Haltwhistle branch.
Lens of Sutton

mineral products by road; thereafter, residual goods services survived at Alston until September 1965.

Inevitably, the Alston branch was marked down for closure during the notorious Beeching period, but in the event the line lingered until the mid-1970s – by which time (claimed BR) it was losing £73,000 a year. In March 1976, few people were surprised by the announcement that all services would cease from Monday 3 May, with the last trains running on Saturday 1 May 1976. As usual, large numbers of extra travellers turned up to see and photograph the last hours – the solemnity of the occasion being accentuated by driving rain of the most dismal kind.

It seemed that the Alston line was destined for ultimate extinction, but happily, local enthusiasts were able to convert a short section of the former trackbed into an interesting narrow gauge tourist railway, and on 30 July 1983 a train service was reintroduced between Alston and a new halt at Gilderdale.

Above:
Class 4MT 2-6-0 No 43121 heads an enthusiasts' special along the Alston branch, near Slaggyford, on 26 March 1967. Note the NER slotted distant signal, seen above the first coach. *John R. P. Hunt*

Left:
Before the removal of its overall roof, Alston station is seen here on 5 September 1962 with the 5.40pm for Haltwhistle awaiting passengers. *L. Sandler*

15

CHAPTER TWO

The Little North Western Line

Running for more than 70 miles between Leeds, in the former West Riding of Yorkshire, and Morecambe, on the Lancashire coast, the Leeds-Morecambe line is a classic trans-Pennine route. Ironically, it was planned not as an east-to-west cross-country line, but as an integral part of a north-to-south trunk route which, if successfully completed, would have carried main line traffic between London and Scotland via Leeds, Ingleton and Carlisle; as such, the line was a precursor of the later Settle and Carlisle line (which branched from the Leeds-Morecambe route at Settle Junction).

Origins of the Little North Western Railway

The scheme originated during the 'Railway Mania' of the 1840s when a group of ambitious industrialists, merchants and local gentlemen sought Parliamentary consent for a 'railway from the Leeds & Bradford Extension Railway to the Lancaster & Carlisle Railway, with diverging lines therefrom . . . to be called the North Western Railway'. A Bill was deposited in the early months of 1846, and strongly supported by the Lancaster & Carlisle Railway, the Leeds & Bradford Railway, and by the inhabitants of Lancaster, Kirkby Lonsdale and Settle. The North Western Railway received the Royal Assent on 26 June 1846.

The Act (9 & 10 Vic. cap 92) provided for construction of a main line from Skipton to a junction with the Lancaster & Carlisle Railway near Low Gill, with a branch running westwards from Clapham to Lancaster; capital of £1,000,000 in £20 shares was authorised, and this trans-Pennine line would be engineered by Charles Vignoles (1793-1874).

Unfortunately, a series of failed corn and potato harvests led to an economic crisis of immense proportions, and in common with most other railway projects at that time, the

Below:
The Little NWR. The Morecambe-Leeds route and connecting lines, 1990.

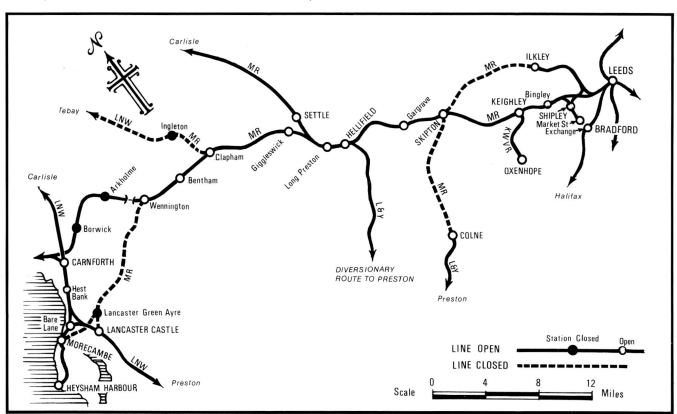

Little North Western soon found itself in serious financial difficulties. Eventually, improved trading conditions enabled construction to slowly proceed, and at a half-year meeting held at Skipton on 22 February 1849 it was reported that, although no satisfactory progress had been made at the Skipton end, the remaining part towards Ingleton was 'almost completed'. On an optimistic note, the directors 'entertained little doubt' that a line from Skipton to Wennington, a distance of 27¾ miles, would be ready for opening by the autumn.

There had, in the difficult years since 1846, been several changes of plan, and in view of their underlying financial problems the promoters decided to concentrate, in the first instance, in the 'branch' to Lancaster. The Little NWR's Consulting Engineer was now Thomas Gooch (1808-1882), with John Watson on site as resident engineer, and the directors included (among others) Pudsey Dawson of Hornby Castle, Edward Sharpe of Lancaster, Henry Anthony Littledale of Bolton Hall, John Waddingham of Leeds, John Rand of Bradford, Hugh Hornby of Liverpool and E. D. Salisbury of Lancaster. Gooch – an elder brother of Daniel Gooch of the GWR – had already carried out much work on the Manchester & Leeds Railway and other local lines, but sadly, overwork caused a breakdown in his health and he is unlikely to have played an active part during the final stages of construction. The main burden of responsibility therefore passed to John Watson, the resident engineer.

Above:
A two-car Class 101 DMU arrives at Morecambe with a morning train from Leeds in September 1979. The glazed roof in the centre covers the spacious concourse. *Howard Quayle*

Opening & Early Years

The first section of the so-called Little NWR was opened from Skipton to Ingleton on 30 July 1849, and in its first months this 25-mile branch was worked as a single line extension of the Leeds & Bradford route from Leeds. The new railway was popular with local travellers, and on 1 September 1849 the *Railway Times* reported that traffic 'already exceeded anything that had been anticipated'.

In the west, a separate section of the route was opened from Lancaster to Wennington on 31 October, though public opening did not apparently take place until 17 November 1849. From Lancaster, trains could reach Poulton (Morecambe) over the metals of the Morecambe Bay Harbour & Railway Company. This last-named section of line, between Morecambe and Lancaster Green

Ayre had been opened as early as 12 June 1848, and although initially a separate company, it was worked by the Little NWR from its inception.

The opening of the Lancaster to Wennington line attracted considerable attention, and the proceedings were covered by the *Illustrated London News*, which printed a full report on 3 November 1849. The report is worth quoting in some detail:

'OPENING OF A PORTION OF THE LANCASTER BRANCH OF THE NORTH WESTERN RAILWAY – This line of railway is not, as many of our southern readers may suppose, one of the many branches or parts of The London and North Western, but an independent line from Skipton, in the West Riding of Yorkshire, to a point of junction on the Lancaster & Carlisle north of Kendal, Westmorland, with a branch from Clapham to the ancient town of Lancaster. From Skipton to Ingleton it is open for traffic; thence to the north the works are for the present suspended. The branch from Clapham to Wennington is in progress, and it is the opening of the portion thence to Lancaster that we have to record.

On Wednesday, the 31st ult. the waving of banners from every coigne of vantage of the Lancaster station, and the important bustling of the officials, gave note of

Below:
Gradient Profile: Leeds to Morecambe.
From **Gradient Profiles M7 & M14**

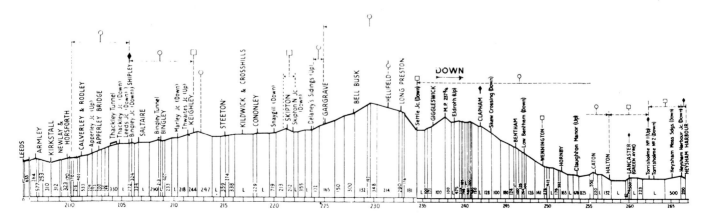

preparation. By one o'clock all was in readiness. The directors and their friends assembled, the fortunate holders of tickets crowding the platform, and the company's engineer, J. Watson, Esq., for the once turned engine-driver, waited for the moment when the numerous party would be safely seated in the cars, to give, by a touch of his hand, motion to a power which would rush on its journey with its living freight swifter than the wind . . . All being arranged – a whistle – and we were off. A very few minutes revealed to us that the country we were traversing was one of no ordinary character or interest.

For the first mile and a half of our journey, a broad, clear river ran on our left hand, and then through the trees we caught passing glimpses of a village on the opposite bank of the stream. This was Halton, in ancient days a place of importance, and a port. Some antiquities still remain here – part of a sculptured Danish cross in the churchyard and a perfect Roman fort. Another mile, and over a timber viaduct we, for the first time, crossed the River Lune; progressed a few hundred yards – and rushed upon another viaduct – and then there burst upon our sight a region of surpassing beauty. Stream and river, hanging woods and mountains steep, embowered village church, rustic mill, and baronial towers all combined to form a picture so perfect of its kind that not in all broad England can be found a scene that surpasses this – the Valley of the Lune. A hill thickly wooded to the summit rises steeply up, and over the topmost trees the turrets of Hornby tower peep out. Behind again, deeply blue, the hill of Ingleborough raises his broad top and closes in the view.

Through this splendid valley, each minute losing beauties and discovering new ones, past Caton (worthy of more length and notice than this) and Claughton, we arrived at Fernley, an ancient seat of the Stanleys. The castle standing on a finely wooded eminence has, by removing a common front and making additions and alterations in keeping with the old part of the structure, been rendered highly picturesque – the owner, Pudsey Dawson, Esq., having escaped the fate of most renovators; he has not spoiled by improving.

At Fernley we left the River Lune, soon crossed the Findburn by a timber viaduct and thence onwards by the Wenning Waterside, past Tatham with its neatly kept graveyard and very white church, and so to Wennington. Here, leaving the train, we walked a short distance to Robert Hall, an ancient edifice formerly the residence of the Cantsfields and once the home of Catherine Parr. It is now utterly neglected. Returning to the train, we were hurried back to Lancaster and thence to the shores of Morecambe Bay, where, in the company's hotel, the directors had provided a repast for the whole of their excursionist friends – a pleasant wind-up to a pleasant day.'

The *Illustrated London News* reporter made no mention of any station buildings (which were probably incomplete) but he was particularly impressed by the long wooden viaduct across the Lune at Lancaster Green Ayre, which was described as follows:

'Carrying a continuation of the line to Poulton, across the River Lune, is a timber viaduct. Spanning the river diagonally, and (to suit the exigencies of the line of which it forms a part) in the form of a segment, it is of a length much greater than the width of the river, being 620 feet overall, and thus combining in itself two features of bridge architecture, which, before the commencement of railway works, were rarely met with, the curve and the skew – the former being in this case one of 500 feet radius and the latter is at an angle of 40 degrees. We believe no other structure has these two features in combination so markedly developed. It has ten openings of 50 feet each, over which the roadway is partly upheld by pile piers and partly suspended from lancinated arches. The piers consist of clustered piles, presenting the least possible obstruction to the flow of water, and having an appearance so light in proportion to the mass they have to support that persons unable to appreciate the strength of a structure acquired by skilful combination of its parts, are apt to arrive at conclusions as to its stability the reverse of true . . . We think no plan can be devised to build a bridge that would be more perfect in its adoption than the present structure. As to proof of its great strength and promise of stability, we may mention that under a pressure of 98 tons concentrated upon one arch, when tested under the inspection of Captain Wynne, Government Inspector, and J. Watson, Esq., CE, the deflection was only ⅝ of an inch.'

The Little NWR route was as yet, still far from complete, and although trains were now running on two separate sections of line, the intervening portion between Wennington and Clapham remained unfinished. On 19 December 1849, however, the railway's supporters were encouraged by the opening of a short connecting line between their station at Lancaster Green Ayre, and the nearby Lancaster & Carlisle line. Little NWR trains were, as a result, able to run in connection with those on the main line, and a 'very satisfactory arrangement' was made for the interchange of traffic at Lancaster.

These promising developments were made known to the rank and file shareholders at the half-year meeting held in February 1850, together with the welcome news that works on the unfinished portion of the line were 'in very advanced state'. Indeed, continued the directors, there was 'every reason to believe' that the entire line from Skipton to Lancaster would be open to traffic by June 1850. The report added that a line like the Little NWR was 'dependent in a great measure for its traffic on two important trunk railways', and in order that 'punctuality and certainty of working' could be achieved, the new line would be doubled throughout from Skipton to Clapham. The second line of rails would cost an additional £45,000, but the directors were so convinced that a double line was an 'absolute necessity' that they were prepared to borrow the extra money on their own personal security, provided that the shareholders would empower them 'to make further calls on the old shares, in the event of their being unable to borrow on the debentures of the company a sufficient amount to repay the loans which may be so obtained'.

Having listened with mixed feelings to the final part of their directors' report, the assembled shareholders then heard a short engineering report prepared by John Watson (who had by this time taken effective charge of the works). The Engineer's Report was as follows:

'In presenting my half-yearly report, I have great pleasure in being able to state that 39 miles of your line are now open for traffic, leaving a link of only eight miles incomplete in the chain connecting the Lancaster & Carlisle Railway at Lancaster, with the Midland Railway at Skipton; and from the present advanced state of the works, I confidently expect that this will be completed within the time stated in the contract, *viz.,* the end of May next. I am now also able to state that the stability of the works (on the portion of the line opened) realises my most sanguine expectations; no failure of any kind has taken place, and I have every reason to expect that you will find the remaining portion of the works as efficiently constructed. The permanent way is in very good working order, and has been well maintained by the contractors. I entirely concur with the recommendation of Mr Gooch, your consulting engineer, as to the propriety of laying down between Skipton and Clapham the second line of rail, respecting which I need not enter into detail, as the matter had been very fully and ably explained by him.

John Watson.'

The line was, as predicted, extended from Wennington to Bentham on 2 May 1850 and completed throughout on 1 June. On that day a through service was inaugurated between Poulton and Leeds, and the branch from Clapham to Ingleton was simultaneously closed — though the Little NWR directors hoped to continue the line northwards from its Ingleton terminus as and when their financial situation improved. In the meantime, the existing route between Poulton, Lancaster, Clapham and Leeds would (it was hoped) generate funds with which the entire scheme could be completed.

In the event, inter-company rivalries ensured that the Little NWR remained of secondary importance, with a service of about three trains each way on its expensive trans-Pennine route. The Little NWR was nevertheless an independent line with many individualistic features; its locomotives, for instance, were named after local buildings or mountains such as *Hornby Castle, Skipton Castle, Lancaster Castle, Whernside* and *Pennighent* (sic). Similarly, its architecture owed little to outside interests, and most of the original intermediate stations were provided with attractive Tudor style timber-framed buildings — which were presumably designed by John Watson.

Subsequent Developments

In 1852, the expansionist Midland Railway assumed control of the line, and in the next few years the route lost much of its individuality. On the other hand the Little NWR company remained in being as a separate entity for many years thereafter, and the final MR takeover did not take place until 1 January 1871.

The Midland made many additions and improvements to the Little NWR and by the end of the 19th century timber bridges had been strengthened or replaced, stations rebuilt, and the entire line had been resignalled with standard MR semaphores controlled from that company's characteristic hip-roofed signal cabins.

The line became surprisingly popular with long-distance commuters, who were able to live at a distance from the smoking mill chimneys of Leeds or Bradford, whilst travelling daily to work in comfortable business expresses. The journey from Poulton (which was officially renamed Morecambe in 1889) to Bradford took about 2hr, and in the years before World War 1 West Riding industrialists were

Left:
Over now-long-vanished metals, Stanier Class 4MT 2-6-4T No 42571 approaches Lancaster Green Ayre with the Morecambe portion of the 1.53pm Leeds City-Carnforth and Morecambe Promenade on 23 June 1962.
Noel A. Machell

Above:
Between Lancaster and Hornby, the now-closed Midland route passed through the attractive lower reaches of the Lune Valley. On 29 September 1964, Class 4F 0-6-0 No 44149 with cover over tender coal space for use with a large plough nears Halton with the 12.40 Heysham-Tees liquid ammonia tank empties, passing over the approach road to the nearby toll bridge.
Noel A. Machell

Left:
Cross-country passenger train: Class 31 No 31440, heading the 13.36 Lancaster-Hull on 11 August 1984, is halted at Wennington, the driver being advised of sheep on the line. The Lancaster line formerly diverged to the left.
Tom Heavyside

Right:
**Cross-country freight: amid pleasant rural scenery, Class 40
No 40169 is halted by adverse signals at Wennington on 27 March
1982, while a Class 104 DMU enters the station with a
Leeds-Morecambe working.** *Tom Heavyside*

Below right:
**The Carnforth-Leeds route has always been popular for steam
specials. On 28 July 1968, BR Standard Class 4MT 4-6-0s
Nos 75019 and 75027 climb the Wenning Valley, between
Bentham and Clapham, with an enthusiasts' excursion returning
to Birmingham.** *Paul Claxton*

able to take advantage of special Club Carriages offering
many extra facilities; a mill owner might, for example,
conduct meetings or read reports during the morning up or
evening down journeys — though many of these upper
middle class travellers would no doubt have preferred to
simply chat or smoke in their comfortable padded
armchairs!

Holiday traffic was not as important in the 19th century
as residential traffic, but as standards of living improved the
railway companies were quick to realise that leisure travel
could be profitable, and many resorts were served by two or
more competing companies. Morecambe was no exception,
and on 16 October 1864 the London & North Western
Railway (LNWR) had opened a branch from Hest Bank on
the nearby West Coast main line. Although initially built as
a connection to Morecambe Harbour, the LNWR line was
soon carrying holiday traffic to and from this growing
resort, and in 1887 a south curve was installed between
Bare Lane and Hest Bank South Junction, in order to
provide a direct link from the south.

In September 1904, the Midland extended its own line
southwards to serve a new harbour at Heysham, from

Below:
**In June 1974, a Class 31 hauls a Heysham-Leeds parcels train
through a deserted Clapham station: the mound of stones marks
the trackbed of the line from Low Gill and Ingleton.**
Stanley Creer

Above:
An interesting Edwardian view of Clapham, showing the ornate mock Tudor station buildings to advantage. *Lens of Sutton*

A Note on Motive Power

The Little NWR line was worked by an interesting range of Midland and LMS locomotive types, including Kirtley 2-4-0s, Midland Compound 4-4-0s, '2P' 4-4-0s, '3F' 0-6-0s, '4F' 0-6-0s, 'Black Five' 4-6-0s, 'Jubilee' 4-6-0s and large 2-6-4Ts such as Fowler or Fairburn 4MTs. Double-heading was not uncommon, and on this hilly route it was possible to see, for example, 'Black Five' or 'Jubilee' 4-6-0s working in conjunction with Fowler 2-6-4Ts. An unusual visitor, around 1950, was a diminutive ex-NER 'Y7' 0-4-0T which was used by Harbour & General Works Ltd during reconstruction work on Morecambe's sea wall. The locomotive involved was former BR No 68089, which ran on a system of temporary contractor's lines — some of which were covered at high tide!

The Route Described

In common with other seaside towns, Morecambe enjoyed lavish rail facilities for many years, but in the 1960s its two routes came under scrutiny. Modest rationalisation followed, and on Saturday 1 January 1966 the Midland line was closed west of Wennington, and all trains were routed via the LNWR line from Hest Bank to Carnforth. The Morecambe to Heysham line lingered on until 1975, but, following the troubles in Northern Ireland, cross-Channel traffic declined so much that passenger trains were withdrawn. Nevertheless, trains still run from Morecambe to Leeds, using the original Little NWR line for at least part of their route. (In 1987 a service of passenger trains was reinstated to and from Heysham in connection with Isle of Man ferry sailings.)

where a fleet of fast turbine steamers ran to and from Northern Ireland; the line was electrified from Heysham to Lancaster in 1908. Morecambe was, by this time, a thriving holiday resort, popular with West Riding holidaymakers who used the line from Leeds to reach their summer playground. The once-prestigious business traffic declined after 1914, but the Little NWR route continued to carry main line trains, including important boat trains from Leeds to Heysham Harbour.

Below left:
Beneath the brooding flat top of Ingleboro' (2,376ft), 'B1' class 4-6-0 No 1306 *Mayflower* and Stanier 4-6-0 No 45407 descend through Eldroth with a Carnforth-Leeds special on 16 October 1976. *Tom Heavyside*

Above:
Diesel restored – Class 40 No 40122/D200 heads the 11-coach 'Cumbrian Mountain Express' on Giggleswick Bank in December 1983. *Les Nixon*

Below:
A four-car Class 101 DMU takes the Morecambe line at Settle Junction, still controlled by an MR signalbox, with the 11.35 from Leeds on 11 September 1981. *Tom Heavyside*

Right:
Ornate ironwork at Hellifield, where the initials 'MR' can clearly be seen in the canopy supports. The wanton neglect of this once fine station is a disgrace to all concerned. *Tom Heavyside*

Left:
In more prosperous times, on 1 May 1967, Class 8F 2-8-0 No 48111 leaves Hellifield, bound for Carlisle via the Settle & Carlisle line. For some years, the steam shed (left) housed some of the National Railway Museum's locomotives. *Les Nixon*

The present Morecambe station was opened in 1907. Two lengthy island platforms are provided, and the station buildings, situated transversely across the western end of the platforms, are of an attractive Gothic design, which look much older than they actually are (railway gothic was rare by the Edwardian period). All goods facilities have been withdrawn, but in general Morecambe Promenade is a terminus little altered by the heavy hand of rationalisation. A particularly pleasing feature is the large wooden signalbox — a hipped-roof structure of perfect Midland design.

In steam days, Morecambe's four terminal roads had their own run-round facilities, and these arrangements included a central engine-release road between Platforms 2 and 3. The goods yard was situated alongside the passenger station, and some of its sidings had originally continued westwards beyond the station area to terminate on a stone pier; these lines (which were lifted in the 1930s) occupied the site of the town's first station. Nearby, the 1930s-style Midland Hotel replaced an original building that had been erected in the 1840s by the Morecambe Bay Harbour & Railway Company.

Leaving Morecambe Promenade, trains pass the connections to Heysham Harbour and the now-lifted Morecambe Bay Harbour & Railway route to Lancaster, while to the left, the site of Euston Road station is now a bus terminal; this former LNWR station was opened in 1886, prior to which all trains had used the nearby Midland terminus. Running now on the 1864 LNWR line, Leeds trains speed past countless villas and guest houses before slowing for the first stop at Bare Lane.

A classic local station, Bare Lane is 1 mile 34 chains from Morecambe, and has up and down platforms, with two-storey, stone-built station buildings on the up side. A manual signalbox stands on the opposite platform, but the traditional gated level crossing has been replaced by full-length lifting barriers. Beyond, the line forks; to the right, a double-track spur turns southwards to join the West Coast main line. This connection is used by Lancaster to Morecambe locals and currently by all Morecambe to Leeds workings, together with freight trains from Heysham, and summer excursion traffic. Northwards, a single-track branch traverses open fields, giving an appearance of rural

tranquility, though this line was, from 1966 until 1982, the main line to West Yorkshire!

Taking the sharply-curved right-hand spur, trains reach the main line at Morecambe South (formerly the Hest Bank South) Junction, then continue south towards Lancaster. A little over a mile further on, the route is carried over the River Lune on the lofty Carlisle Bridge, which is the third to occupy the site. The original Lancaster & Carlisle viaduct had been of mainly wooden construction, but this was replaced by a second bridge in 1866; the present structure was erected in 1962-63, and consists of modern reinforced-concrete spans resting upon the 1866 piers.

As their train rumbles across the Lune, observant travellers can, by glancing downwards, see the course of the abandoned Midland line on the north bank of the river. To the east, the former Little NWR bridge (rebuilt by the MR in 1864 and again in 1912) now carries an incessant stream of road traffic, while Green Ayre station — on the south bank of the Lune — has been obliterated by modern roadworks. Having crossed Carlisle Bridge, trains come to rest in the shadow of Lancaster's brooding, heavily-machicolated medieval castle — which occupies a prominent hilltop position to the east of the railway.

Lancaster station is 4 miles 1 chain from Morecambe Promenade; formerly known as Lancaster Castle to distinguish it from neighbouring Green Ayre, it is one of the most attractive stations on the West Coast main line (WCML). First opened in 1846, Castle station originally had just two through platforms for up and down main line traffic, but changes carried out at the end of the 19th century resulted in a much enlarged layout, with four through platforms and two dead-end bays at the northernmost end of the main down platform.

Architecturally, the station's ornate Gothic buildings are of particular interest; the oldest portion is on the down side, but its original appearance has been partially obscured by later additions and by a wide covered footbridge that extends horizontally from a separate high-level booking office on the up side. To the north, the towering Lancaster No 4 signalbox (now demolished) controlled the northern end of the station layout — including a steeply-graded connection which descended abruptly towards the Little NWR station at Green Ayre. The box itself was a typical

LNWR design, similar to scores of others throughout the former LNWR system.

After a suitable pause, trains reverse at Lancaster Castle, and then retrace their course northwards as far as Morecambe South Junction. Beyond, the route continues beneath the wires to Carnforth (10 miles 8 chains) where the main line platforms were demolished during the WCML electrification. A gloomy, stone-built station, Carnforth was the setting for several scenes in the famous postwar British film classic *Brief Encounter*, which starred Trevor Howard and Celia Johnson as illicit lovers, able to meet only in a railway refreshment room. In more recent years, Carnforth has become well known as the site of one of Britain's many steam museums — housed in the former BR loco sheds to the west of the station.

Having stopped briefly in the sharply-curved Barrow-in-Furness platforms, Leeds trains negotiate a south-to-east curve which lifts them above the level of the main line to reach the former Furness & Midland Joint Railway (F&M), by means of which eastbound workings can rejoin the Little NWR at Wennington. Opened on 6 June 1867, the F&M runs through pleasant, tree-dotted countryside for 9½ miles. The intermediate stations at Borwick, Arkholme and Melling were closed in September 1960, but observant travellers will spot substantial remains as their trains rush past. At Arkholme, for example, a range of gabled stone buildings survive intact on the up side, having been tastefully converted into a private dwelling. Nearing Wennington the railway passes through a 1,230yd tunnel before the F&M converges with the Little NWR.

Wennington (19 miles 63 chains from Morecambe) is an unstaffed halt, its red brick buildings demolished and its sidings lifted; an item of interest, however, is a small turntable well, isolated in the middle of a nearby farmyard! Until rationalisation, Wennington had been a relatively complex station, with up and down platforms for main line trains, and additional platforms for local traffic on the down side. The main booking office and waiting rooms were on the up platform, and there was a small waiting shelter on the local platform; the goods yard was to the east of the passenger station, on the up side of the line.

From Wennington, the double-track railway climbs towards its summit, crossing and recrossing the sparkling River Wenning on a succession of impressive bridges and viaducts, and passing the invisible borderline between Lancashire and Yorkshire.

Top:
On a wintry day in February 1987, Class 7P 4-6-2 No 6201 *Princess Elizabeth* heads a motley collection of stock northwards over the infant River Aire at Gargrave. *Tom Heavyside*

Above:
Despite service reductions, Skipton survives virtually unchanged: note the splendid glass canopies. A Class 142 DMU departs on the 12.31 Leeds-Lancaster, while other Pacers can be seen in the background. *Tom Heavyside*

Bentham, the next stop, has BR concrete buildings, overshadowed by a large mill to the north of the railway. Still climbing, the line continues eastwards along the Wenning Valley, and Clapham, 3 miles 25 chains further on, is a bleak, lonely place, surrounded by bare, windswept fells. Sadly, the attractive timber-framed station buildings here have been partially demolished, leaving the former stationmaster's house, on the up platform, as a private dwelling. Now an unstaffed halt, devoid of all sidings and connections, Clapham was formerly the junction for branch services to Ingleton.

Right:
1950s period piece: ex-LMS Class 4P 'Compound' 4-4-0 No 41094 approaches Skipton with a Bradford Forster Square – Morecambe Promenade excursion on 20 April 1957. *C. P. Boocock*

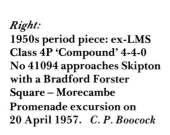

In its Edwardian heyday, the station enjoyed through coaches from the LNWR via Tebay, and in the summer months the 10.00am Leeds-Glasgow and 10.30 Edinburgh-St Pancras were diverted through Clapham and Ingleton. In general, however, the Ingleton route was under-utilised; indeed, as pointed out above, it was closed in 1850 — and not reopened until the completion of a northwards continuation to Tebay (under LNWR auspices) in August 1861. Despite its junction status, Clapham had no bays or other special terminal facilities, though there were several extra sidings in its small goods yard. The signalbox (now demolished) was a standard MR hip-roofed cabin which was known — somewhat confusingly — as Clapham Junction.

Reaching its summit near the unstaffed halt at Giggleswick (32 miles 70 chains) the railway falls towards the Settle-Carlisle main line at Settle Junction, where a modernised ladder crossover has replaced the traditional double-track junction; as a result, Leeds trains run southwards on the down main line for a short distance before crossing over to the up line.

Long Preston, the first station beyond the junction, is another unstaffed halt, with glass bus stop shelters on both platforms, and Hellifield (38 miles 40 chains) is a scene of complete desolation, its stone-built station buildings standing boarded and derelict on a windswept island platform, surrounded by rusting PW sidings. In happier times, the station provided employment for around 60 railwaymen, including clerks, guards, shunters, PW men and locomotive crews. To the south of the platform, the former Lancashire & Yorkshire line to Blackburn is still occasionally used by diverted passenger trains during

Right:
With the Bradford line diverging on the left, a Leeds-Skipton local DMU avoids Shipley on 10 July 1977. Note the commodious station buildings in the centre background. *Les Nixon*

Below:
Midland signalposts, complete with finials, dominate this view of the Aire Valley line at Guiseley Junction, Shipley, taken on 16 September 1978. A Class 108 DMU climbs away from the main line with the 09.38 Bradford-Ilkley. *Les Nixon*

Sunday engineering work on the WCML (see Chapter Five). Departing from Hellifield, trains rush past the closed station at Bell Busk, then pause at Gargrave where, at the time of writing, the original Little NWR timber-framed buildings remain intact on the up platform.

Following the Aire Valley, the trains soon reach Skipton (48¼ miles). Since Carnforth, the line has been very much a 'basic railway', but Skipton is still fully staffed, with interesting stone buildings and extensive glass and iron canopies; there are four platforms including a dead-end bay, and an oil depot beyond the passenger station provides bulk freight traffic. Traditional features here include a private refreshment room and two standard Midland-style signal cabins; a subway connects the up and down platforms at their western end.

Southeastwards, the double-track railway follows the River Aire to Keighley where connection is made with Keighley & Worth Valley Railway (K&WVR) services to Oxenhope. The rather cramped, four-platform station here is divided between BR and the K&WVR, giving excellent interchange facilities. Opened on 13 April 1867, the Worth Valley line was closed to all traffic in June 1962, subsequently reopening as a private line on 29 June 1968. A

noticeable feature of the branch is the very tightly curved, rising gradient out of Keighley station, which calls for skilful driving if excessive wheelslip is to be avoided.

The landscape on this final section of the Morecambe-Leeds line is dramatic, with immense textile mills crowding on to the railway on all sides; there are some particularly fine examples around Bingley (50¼ miles) where the Victorian industrialist Sir Titus Salt created his model factory settlement at Saltaire between 1851 and 1876. When first built, Saltaire was situated amidst green fields, and its two-platform station was not opened until 1859.

The original Saltaire station was closed in 1965 and its attractive Italianate station buildings were subsequently demolished, but on 9 April 1984 a new halt was opened on the old site, and taking advantage of an EEC grant, BR and the West Yorkshire County Planning Department decided to build a distinctly 'Midland' style station, with diagonal-pattern fencing and traditional stone-built waiting shelters. Unusually, the new stopping place was given ornate 'Victorian' platform lamps, and uninitiated travellers find it hard to believe that the present Saltaire station is (apart from one stone stairway) an entirely modern, BR-built halt.

Left:
A turn-of-the-century poster advertising some of the many attractive places served by the Midland Railway.

track and signal work, both up and down main line trains started to call here, eastbound workings running 'wrong line' to do so. Amusingly, Shipley station is now a perfect triangle, with platforms on all three sides! Accelerating away from Shipley, trains pass a former GNR station building, which survives more or less intact on the southern side of the line.

Approaching Leeds, the trains pass a classic roundhouse style locomotive shed on the left-hand side of the line (now used for industrial purposes). Finally, some 75 miles from Morecambe, the diesel multiple-units (DMUs) come to rest in the large modern station at Leeds, where connections are available for London King's Cross, York and a variety of other destinations in both the North and South of England. Opened on 17 May 1967, the present station has seven terminal bays and five long through platforms, while, to the north, additional bays are available for parcels traffic.

The 1985 timetable provided seven eastbound and six westbound trains between Leeds, Morecambe and Lancaster, each service taking, on average, around 2hr for their trans-Pennine journeys. Until the closure of Heysham station in May 1975 one of the eastbound morning trains had connected with an overnight Sealink service from Belfast, while in the opposite direction an evening departure from Leeds connected with the night sailing to Northern Ireland; additional boat trains traditionally ran during the summer months, and there was, at one time, a connecting service to Dublin (Dun Laoghaire).

The current timetables reflect changes carried out in 1982 when, as a result of downgrading on the Settle-Carlisle line, several locomotive-hauled trains were routed to the WCML via Leeds and Lancaster. By September 1985 all locomotive-hauled trains had reverted to multiple-unit operation, with an intermediate call at Lancaster en route to Morecambe. The situation is, at present, in a state of flux, and the future pattern of operation on the Little NWR line is difficult to predict with any degree of certainty.

Below:
Class 9F 2-10-0 No 92234 storms through the closed Apperley Bridge station with Barrow-Monckton coal empties on 23 March 1967. *Les Nixon*

Bingley, Saltaire and Shipley are practically contiguous, and after a century of urban growth the area now forms one built-up conurbation. Shipley station is similar to that at Bingley, and both stations have Gothic style architecture. In the mid-1960s, Leeds trains started to reverse here, as the station is situated south of the main line on a branch to Bradford. (Hitherto, numerous Bradford-Leeds workings had given Shipley travellers a good service to and from Leeds, but with the relative demise of the line to Bradford Forster Square, these services had proved insufficient.) In 1979, BR belatedly opened a single platform on the direct Morecambe-Leeds line, and in 1980, following appropriate

CHAPTER THREE

The Settle & Carlisle Railway

The Little NWR was in effect an extension of the Leeds & Bradford line and it should, as such, have given the Midland Railway (MR) an outlet to the north which (in normal circumstances) would have provided that company with a main line to Scotland. Unfortunately, the entire scheme was dependent upon LNWR co-operation — the line from Ingleton northwards being under the control of Euston. For its part, the LNWR showed little inclination to smooth the path of Midland ambitions, and the arrangements at Ingleton were therefore made as awkward as possible; through services were (in the 1850s and 1860s) out of the question, and Midland travellers were obliged to change at both Ingleton and Tebay. The entire exercise was clearly designed to frustrate the Midland, and in this situation it was inevitable that, sooner or later, the MR would seek to circumvent the LNWR route by building an entirely new main line to Carlisle. Thus, in 1866 — in the midst of the second 'Railway Mania' — the company lodged a Bill for the construction of the spectacular Settle-Carlisle Railway.

An Unnecessary Scheme?

The Settle & Carlisle scheme was surrounded by controversy from its very inception, and at a time when the Midland was heavily committed to new construction elsewhere, many MR shareholders were understandably alarmed at the prospect of yet another expensive main line. These doubts were forcibly aired during the company's half-year meeting, held at Derby in February 1866; the Chairman, William Evans Hutchinson, reported that work on the Midland extensions to Buxton, London and other places was progressing, and there were hopes that the 'Bedford and London would be opened for goods and mineral traffic in the autumn of next year'. He next outlined the various new projects before Parliament, which he was sorry to say were numerous. These included lines to Malvern (which the Midland hoped to lease), new works in Yorkshire, and the Ashby & Nuneaton line in Leicestershire. Mr Hutchinson said a few words about these new projects, before turning to the 'Bill for enabling the company to make a railway from Settle to Carlisle'.

The new railway would be about 72 miles long, and would cost an estimated £368,000; for this modest sum, the Midland would be placed in connection with the North British, Caledonian, Glasgow & South Western, North Eastern, and Maryport & Carlisle systems. There would be 'a considerable local traffic', and the traffic between England and Scotland 'was very large and increasing every year'. At present, continued the Chairman, this Anglo-Scottish traffic flowed over the rival LNWR or Great Northern systems, and 'very little' found its way on to the Midland — although the latter had a system of its own 'from London to Ingleton, within about 60 miles of Carlisle'.

Below:
Gradient Profile: Settle & Carlisle line.
From **Gradient Profiles** *LM7*

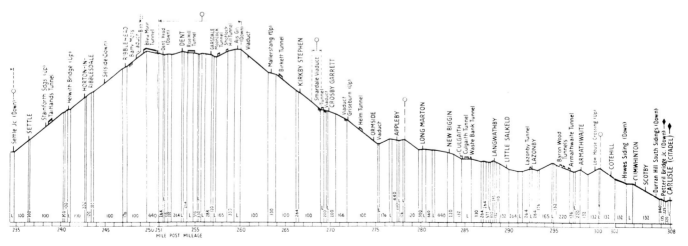

The Chairman argued that the Midland was entitled to a much *larger* share of the Scottish traffic than it presently received, and the new Settle to Carlisle line would ensure that a significant proportion of this traffic reached its own line, making it 'one of the great main arteries commencing at London and terminating at Carlisle'. With regard to the financial outlay, added Mr Hutchinson, there would be a small outlay necessary for the commencement of 'a tunnel and some heavy cuttings', but otherwise the main burden would fall when 'the Bedford and London, and other important works, were producing a revenue'.

Having listened intently to the Chairman's report, the Midland shareholders soon made their own views known, a Mr Hadley being particularly vociferous in his condemnation of continual expenditure on expensive new works. At this point other shareholders complained of time wasting, but Mr Hadley refused to sit down until he had read a prepared statement. The Chairman then complained that it was a great pity that individuals with 'an insignificant stake in the concern should habitually occupy the largest share of the time given to their meetings', but this remark served only to raise the ire of other shareholders who claimed that the Chairman had made an impertinent remark to Mr Hadley. With the entire meeting degenerating into farce, Mr Hadley stood his ground, adding that he thought it 'premature to make a Settle and Carlisle line'. Another shareholder — managing to get a word in — claimed that the Great Western and Great Eastern companies had been 'ruined' by borrowing money to make unnecessary branch lines, and it soon became painfully clear that many Midland proprietors were bitterly opposed to the entire Settle & Carlisle scheme.

The Bill, meanwhile, was progressing through Parliament, and despite strenuous opposition from the LNWR, the Settle & Carlisle scheme received its Royal Assent on 16 July 1866. The resulting Act (29 & 30 Vic. cap 223) provided for construction of an 80-mile main line; for convenience, the authorised route was treated as three distinct lines, the first of which would be:

'A railway twenty-eight miles and one furlong or thereabouts in length, to commence in the Parish of Giggleswick and township of Settle in the West Riding of the County of York, by a junction with the North Western Railway, and terminating in the Parish of Aysgarth and township of Hawes in the North Riding of the County of York.'

The next portion of the line would form an end-on junction with this railway, and would be:

'A railway twenty-five miles five furlongs four chains and fifty links or thereabouts in length, to commence in the Parish of Sedburgh . . . by a junction with the intended railway hereinbefore described, and terminating in the Parish of Saint Martin Appleby . . .'

Finally, the northernmost part of the route would comprise:

'A railway twenty-nine miles five furlongs and five chains or thereabouts in length, to commence in the Parish of Saint Martin Appleby . . . by a junction with the intended Railway hereinbefore described, and terminating in the Parish of Saint Cuthberts Carlisle, in the County of Cumberland, by a junction with the main lines of the Newcastle and Carlisle Railway of the North Eastern Railway Company on the east side of the River Petteril.'

The Midland was given running powers over the NER and into Carlisle Citadel station, and additional share and loan capital of £2,000,000 was authorised to pay for the new main line. In the event, the project was destined to cost some £3 million — a figure which the redoubtable Mr Hadley had earlier predicted.

In September 1866 the line was staked out for much of its length, but there was no attempt to begin construction. This was, at least in part, a reflection of the Midland's

Above:
A typical Settle & Carlisle freight – Class 45 No 45004 *Royal Irish Fusilier* heads north past Horton sidings with a Healey Mills-Carlisle freight on 25 July 1979. *Tom Heavyside*

financial problems in the wake of the sudden failure of bankers Overend & Gurney in the previous May; it had become increasingly difficult to raise capital for new schemes and the MR directors may have decided to postpone construction until the overall business climate became more congenial. On the other hand, it is possible that the whole Settle & Carlisle scheme was a gigantic bluff designed to bring the LNWR to the negotiating table *vis-à-vis* Ingleton and the Anglo-Scottish traffic. If this was indeed the case the ploy was highly successful, and the hitherto unhelpful LNWR (alarmed by the nightmare prospect of a rival trunk route just a few miles to the east of

Above left:
On 21 July 1976, Class 40 No 40003 approaches the junction with the Carnforth line, heading an up fitted freight. *Tom Heavyside*

Left:
Traffic now diverted – Class 47 No 47318 heads a company train, northwards from Settle up the Ribble Valley on 5 September 1979. *Les Nixon*

Right:
The end of through services from the south – on the last day of these workings (15 May 1982), Class 47 No 47535 *University of Leicester* heads the 09.41 Leicester-Glasgow near Stainforth. *Tom Heavyside*

construction of the Settle & Carlisle — an expensive white elephant which, by 1869, the company no longer wanted!

Construction of the S&C

Construction of the 72-mile long main line proceeded simultaneously from several different points, and various engineering firms were involved in the work, including Messrs Benton & Woodiwiss, Joseph Firbank, and John Ashwell of London. Some of these firms, such as Firbanks, were highly respected civil engineering contractors of international repute. Others — among them Benton & Woodiwiss — had successfully carried out work on the Furness and other local lines, but Ashwell was apparently a smaller contractor with less experience of major railway works.

John Crossley (1812-78), the Midland's Engineer, exercised overall control of the works, while stations and other architectural features were the responsibility of I. H. Saunders, the Company Architect.

The authorised route was unique in that, unlike other Pennine railways, it did not pass from west to east through some convenient cleft or valley — it followed the mountains longitudinally, on an approximate north-south alignment that left little scope for economy or ease of construction. There were nevertheless two north-south valleys which, between them, offered a feasible path; from Settle the upper Ribble Valley extended northwards, while from the Carlisle end the Eden Valley provided a corresponding routeway towards the south. The problems centred on an intervening area of high moorland, through which the railway builders would have to hack and blast their way before the Ribble and Eden Valleys could be united. This remote, desolate spot was known — appropriately — as Blea Moor; its average elevation was well over 1,000ft and major tunnels and other civil engineering works were inevitable.

For seven years, armies of navvies struggled to build the line, and as they toiled amid the bleak moors, costs

its own line) sued for peace. With a better deal on the table, the Midland directors decided to abandon the Settle & Carlisle project, but when the necessary Abandonment Bill was sent up to Parliament in 1869, it faced bitter opposition from other railways — notably the Lancashire & Yorkshire and North British companies, both of which had welcomed the Settle & Carlisle as a means of breaking the existing LNWR monopoly south of Carlisle. Parliament also saw the virtues of competition, and the Abandonment Bill was thrown out; the Midland was thereby obliged to begin

mounted inexorably; Blea Moor Tunnel presented particular problems, and John Ashwell, its unfortunate contractor, was driven to bankruptcy. Elsewhere, areas of unstable, peaty soil swallowed whole embankments — at Dandry Mire, for example, material was tipped for two years, and in the end it was necessary to build a viaduct in lieu of the planned earthworks; accidents were frequent, with an average of perhaps one death a week among the navvies. The men themselves came from all parts of the British Isles, and in the absence of proper accommodation at places such as Blea Moor they lived in 'Wild West' type shanty towns with names like Sebastopol, Jerusalem and Salt Lake City!

Opening of the Line

Eventually, after much expenditure of time and blood, the new railway at last began to take shape in the primeval moorlands, and in February 1876 the works were inspected by Col Rich of the Board of Trade. The Inspector took

several days to cover the entire line, but was unable to pass the Settle & Carlisle for passenger traffic. His report nevertheless contains an interesting first-hand account of the line; there were, for example, no less than 25 viaducts, together with 85 overbridges and 150 underbridges, and 13 tunnels. The permanent way was formed of 80lb rails, resting in 40lb cast iron chairs which were in turn attached to conventional cross sleepers; 15 of the stations were more or less complete, but they required clocks, nameboards, lamps and other necessary fittings. More seriously, the line needed additional catch points, and its drainage works were incomplete.

In the meantime, it seems that the line was already open for at least some forms of freight traffic, and a report printed in *The Railway Times* mentioned that goods traffic had commenced on 1 August 1875. Curiously, this would have been a Sunday, and it is perhaps more likely that the paper intended to say that freight working would begin in the *month* of August — in which case it is more likely that traffic commenced on the following Monday (ie 2 August 1875).

Top:
The grandeur of Pen-y-Ghent (2,278ft) dominates this view of Class 40 No 40032 *Empress of Canada* **heading south towards Selside with an up freight on 21 July 1976.** *Tom Heavyside*

Right:
Across the top of the Pennines – on 31 March 1984, a Class 47 crosses Ribblehead Viaduct with a southbound special working. Note the repair scaffolding on the extreme left-hand arches.
Tom Heavyside

The Board of Trade Inspector returned in April, and finally, on the 25th of that month he belatedly passed the Settle & Carlisle route for passenger traffic. A week later, on 1 May 1876, the line was ceremonially opened, the official 'first train' being a long-distance special from London St Pancras to Glasgow St Enoch. A few hours earlier, Kirtley 2-4-0 No 806 had hauled the first public service over the line; this historic working had been driven by John Mayblin of Carlisle.

Although the new main line was at last in operation, it was still in many ways incomplete, with several stations still under construction. Despite this deficiency, the Settle & Carlisle was a spectacular example of Victorian engineering, and contemporary observers were immediately struck by the scale of its works and the awe-inspiring beauty of the surrounding moors. A reporter from the *Sheffield & Rotherham Independent* was particularly impressed, and his description of the line is given below:

'At Settle there is now a junction, whence the new line proceeds, nearly north, but with a westerly inclination, to Carlisle . . . You go up for 15 miles, rising 1 in 100, with only a very few short intervals of easier gradients. Then you are about 1,000 feet higher than Leeds from which you started, and from Carlisle to which you are bound, but as you have made three-fourths of the ascent in the 15 miles from Settle Junction to the top, where you enter Blea Moor Tunnel, you will be aware it is a pretty sharp ascent. Still, it is not nearly so bad as that faced by the passengers on the Lancaster and Carlisle, where there are considerable lengths of 1 in 70, a far more serious thing than the 1 in 100 of the Midland. From Blea Moor Tunnel you run 10 miles along the ridge . . . before the descent northwards begins. Within these 10 miles you pass through two tunnels (the first a mile and a half long and the second of about three-quarters of a mile), and over several wonderful viaducts. During these 10 miles there are intervals of level running.

'In the rest of the 10 miles the gradients are from 1 in 264 to 1 in 440, with two stiffer bits of 1 in 120 and 1 in 165. The 10 miles we have spoken of end at Ais Gill, where there is half a mile of level running, and here is the literal summit of the line. The rails are a few feet higher than at Blea Moor Tunnel.

'The descent on the north side of the hill almost exactly coincides with the ascent on the south side. From the summit level at Ais Gill you go down 15 miles to Ormside, and are there almost at exactly the same level as when you started at Settle Junction to ascend the 15 miles to the Blea Moor Tunnel. From Ormside you descend by a wavy line, no gradient being worse than 1 in 100, and most of the gradients being very much better, till you reach the Petterill Junction with the Newcastle and Carlisle three-quarters of a mile from the Citadel station at Carlisle.'

The reporter noted that, for much of its length, the new railway ran through moorlands covered not by heather, but with 'luxuriant' grass which provided pasturage for 'numerous flocks of sheep' — there would therefore be at least some agricultural traffic. At its northernmost end the Settle & Carlisle line traversed richer, better cultivated land in which rapid advances in cultivation were being made; the inhabitants of the Eden Valley would, it was hoped, 'be excellent customers for a railway'. Of equal promise were the local mineral deposits which held out the promise of profitable exploitation now that the railway was in operation:

'For miles upon miles the railway sides give token of the labour by which it has been made. Yard by yard the rocks have been blasted. But every breach that has been made in the strata reveals subterranean treasures, and has made them easy to get and easy to transport, thus opening to the view future traffic. The Craven Lime

Below:
The scale of Ribblehead Viaduct is shown to good effect in this November 1984 photograph of Class 5MT 4-6-0 No 45407 at the head of the northbound 'Cumbrian Mountain Express'.
Tom Heavyside

Left:
Green-liveried Class 40 No 40122/D200 emerges from the northern portal of Blea Moor Tunnel with 'Knotty Northern Circular' railtour of 7 April 1984. *Tom Heavyside*

Below:
At 1,145ft Dent station is the highest on any English main line. Here ex-Southern Railway 'N15' 4-6-0 No 777 *Sir Lamiel* storms through on the southbound 'Cumbrian Mountain Pullman' on 22 May 1982. *Tom Heavyside*

Company, near Settle, has taken time by the forelock, and is the precursor of many similar undertakings. On the other side of the hill gypsum is ground and transported by the railway to a considerable extent. A reddish stone, like that of the Rother Valley, is abundant at various parts, notably at Lazonby; and the station at Little Salkeld shows a happy combination of the white stone and the red, both found near. The Batty Moss Viaduct is built of black marble. It is obtainable in very large blocks, and its character is said to resemble the Kilkenny rather than the Derbyshire marble. A commencement has also been made in the working of slate quarries.'

The completed railway was, by any definition, a major feat of civil engineering, and having been built at a relatively late date, it exemplified Victorian construction methods at their best. For mile after mile the raw new earthworks scythed through the landscape, and there was both confidence and technical maturity in every station, bridge or tunnel mouth; the Settle & Carlisle had been built by a nation at the height of its power, and there was an imperial grandeur about this new railway and its massive arched viaducts — which were at least the equal of anything created by ancient Rome.

The line was designed as an integral part of an important north-to-south trunk route, and although, at the time of

opening, there were 17 intermediate stations between Settle and Carlisle, these diverse stopping places were not expected to generate significant passenger or freight traffic. Each station followed the same basic plan, having up and down platforms with solid, gabled station buildings on one side and smaller waiting rooms on the other. Few of the stations were provided with goods sheds though (as in indication of the kind of heavy through freight traffic that was expected) there were ample numbers of running loops and refuge sidings into which loose coupled coal or mineral trains could be shunted.

Settle, Kirkby Stephen and Appleby were given slightly larger stations with goods sheds and various other additional facilities, but in general most Settle & Carlisle stations featured relatively simple track layouts with just one or two goods sidings and up/down refuge roads; Dent, Horton-in-Ribblesdale and Ribblehead were typical of these smaller intermediate stations.

Settle & Carlisle Motive Power

The Settle & Carlisle line has, over the years, been worked by an interesting range of (mainly) Midland locomotive types including — in the early days — Kirtley '800' class 2-4-0s, Johnson '1282' class 2-4-0s, Johnson '60' class, '999' class and 'Belpaire' class 4-4-0s and Deeley '990' class

Left:
**In LMS days, 'Royal Scot' 4-6-0 No 6103 *Royal Scots Fusilier*
curves through Doddenham Cutting, at the approach to Dent
station, with an up express.** *Bertram Unne*

Below:
**The Settle & Carlisle in the 1980s – on 30 May 1983, Class 31
No 31207 emerges from Rise Hill Tunnel and approaches Dent
with a Carlisle-Leeds working.** *Tom Heavyside.*

4-4-0s. Freight traffic was handled by successive generations of Midland or LMS goods engines, including Kirtley 0-6-0s, Johnson 0-6-0s and Fowler '3F' and '4F' 0-6-0s. The famous Midland 'Compound' 4-4-0s enjoyed a particularly long association with the route, while in the post-Grouping period former LNWR 'Claughton' 4-6-0s heralded the age of large engines on this hilly, mountain line.

In more recent years, the 'Thames-Clyde Express' and other prestige Settle & Carlisle workings were headed by 'Jubilee' or rebuilt 'Royal Scot' class 4-6-0s, with the impressive 138-ton 1Co-Co1 'Peak' class assuming command in the diesel era. Other classes seen on the line in recent years included 'Black Five' 4-6-0s, Stanier or 'Austerity' 2-8-0s, Standard Class 9F 2-10-0s, Class 40 1Co-Co1s, Class 31 A1A-A1As, and Class 47 Co-Cos. A brief survey of some of the most characteristic Settle & Carlisle locomotive types is given in Table 2 (below).

Table 1
Typical Settle & Carlisle Motive Power 1876-1987

Type	Wheel arrangement	Notes
Kirtley '800' class	2-4-0	Used in the Victorian period
Johnson '1282' class	2-4-0	Used in the Victorian period
Johnson '60' class	4-4-0	
Johnson '999' class	4-4-0	
Johnson 'Belpaire' class	4-4-0	Later designated Class 3
Johnson Compound class	4-4-0	
Deeley Compound class	4-4-0	
Deeley '990' class	4-4-0	
Kirtley	0-6-0	
Johnson 2F	0-6-0	
Johnson/Fowler 3F	0-6-0	
Fowler 4F	0-6-0	
Claughton class	4-6-0	Appeared after Grouping
Jubilee '6P5F' class	4-6-0	
Rebuilt 'Royal Scot' 7P class	4-6-0	
Stanier 8F	2-8-0	
Stanier 'Black Five' Class 5MT	4-6-0	
Standard Class 5MT	4-6-0	
Standard Class 9F	2-10-0	
Gresley Class A3	4-6-2	
Peak Classes 44, 45 & 46	1Co-Co1	
Class 40	1Co-Co1	
Class 50	Co-Co	Appeared on diverted WCML services
Class 47	Co-Co	
Class 31	A1A-A1A	
Class 24	Bo-Bo	
Class 25	Bo-Bo	

(It should be stressed that this list is by no means exhaustive, and many other types of locomotive have appeared, particularly in recent years when railtours have brought Class 55s, 'A4s' and other unlikely visitors on to the Settle-Carlisle route.)

Settle & Carlisle Architecture

Unlike many other lines, the Settle to Carlisle route was built in one short period of time, and for this reason its architecture is surprisingly uniform in relation to many other parts of BR. Apart from Culgaith (which was opened later than the other stations) the 'standard' Settle & Carlisle station building was a rectangular structure measuring approximately 50ft×28ft at ground level.

Viewed from the platform, these characteristic buildings appeared to be conventional 'H' plan structures incorporating a central booking hall and two cross wings, but in fact

the projecting gables were not true cross wings and there were no corresponding gables at the rear; instead, the Settle & Carlisle design provided a single, centrally-sited gable with a deeply-recessed window. There was no rear access (although the rear gable could easily have formed a convenient porch). The gap between the two front gables was occupied by a small wood and glass screen, behind which a pair of double doors gave access to the booking hall; to the right, another door opened on to a general waiting room, while a similar door in the left-hand wing provided access to the ladies' waiting room. At the left of the ladies' room, a 25ft long extension contained the gentlemen's urinal and also provided additional storage space for coal and other items.

When first opened, it seems that all of the Settle & Carlisle stations had ornate barge boards and complex, decorative glazing, but subsequent repairs and alterations introduced countless minor variations between otherwise identical buildings. At Horton-in-Ribblesdale, for instance, the original glazing was replaced by simple, linear glazing bars, while both Horton and Ribblehead lacked the decorative barge boards found at Dent, Settle and elsewhere.

The large, gabled goods sheds at Settle, Kirkby Stephen and Appleby were built in the same architectural style as the station buildings, and several of the bigger stations were equipped with distinctive, Midland-style water towers — that at Appleby being of brick construction whereas most other examples were of local stone. Equally characteristic were the small, subsidiary waiting rooms found at each intermediate stopping place; these were, like the main buildings, gabled structures which, if not overtly Gothic, exuded a faintly ecclesiastical air. All of these buildings are believed to have been designed by I. H. Saunders, the Midland Railway architect.

The line was, from its inception, signalled with the latest Midland-style semaphore signals which were controlled from the company's standard, weather-boarded signal cabins. Although such cabins were erected by the MR Signals and Telegraph Department (and were, therefore, unlikely to be influenced by aesthetic considerations) they were nevertheless distinctive buildings which, like the architect-designed stations, contributed to the overall Settle & Carlisle scene. The boxes were formed of 12ft

Left:
On the final few yards of the climb to Ais Gill Summit, Class 31 No 31226 heads the 15.37 Carlisle-Leeds on a sunny day in May 1982. *Tom Heavyside*

Right:
Steam working on BR is nearly at an end, as grimy 'Britannia' 4-6-2 No 70031 *Byron* crosses Mallerstang Common with a southbound freight. *Les Nixon*

Centre right:
Photographers record one of the final Class 6P5F 'Jubilee' 4-6-0s No 45562 *Alberta*, passing Kirkby Stephen with a Carlisle-bound freight in April 1967. The Midland box was replaced by a new BR structure a year or two later. *Les Nixon*

Below:
'Foreign' motive power on the Settle & Carlisle — station staff at Appleby West watch the passage of the up 'Thames-Clyde Express', powered by grimy Gresley 'A3' class 4-6-2 No 60092 *Fairway* on 23 July 1960. *F. Anderson*

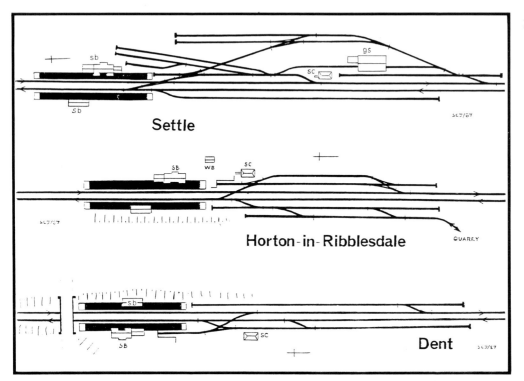

Left:
Trackplans: Settle, Horton-in-Ribblesdale and Dent, c1960.

Settle

Horton-in-Ribblesdale

Dent

prefabricated sections, most examples being two bays long with a total length of about 27ft and a width of 14ft. When new, each box had a hipped, grey slate roof, but later rebuildings inevitably produced several anomalies — Kirkby Stephen, for example, acquired a flat-roofed modern cabin, while Appleby's signalbox was a non-standard, gabled design. In general however, Settle & Carlisle architecture is unusually cohesive, and the design of the line's stations, signalboxes and goods sheds are one of its most attractive features.

The Route Described

Built as a competitive Anglo-Scottish main line, the Settle & Carlisle railway lost much of its *raison d'être* when the rival Midland and London & North Western companies became part of the newly-created London Midland & Scottish (LMS) Railway in 1923. Thereafter, the expensively-engineered Midland route to Scotland settled down to become a freight and secondary line — the main LMS route to Scotland being the nearby WCML.

Despite its obvious utility as an emergency route, the Settle & Carlisle railway had long been a closure candidate. The majority of intermediate stations were closed in 1970 and by 1982; only a residual Leeds-Carlisle service remained. All important long-distance services such as the 'Thames-Clyde Express' having been either diverted or abandoned. The unexpected reprieve for the S&C in April 1989 following a long battle against closure (see Chapter Eight) mean that this impressive trans-Pennine

Below left:
Hard work is reflected in the scorched smokebox door of 'West Country' Class 4-6-2 No 34092 *City of Wells* as it stands at Appleby with the southbound Cumbrian Mountain Pullman on 20 November 1982. *Tom Heavyside*

Below:
The Pennine mountains form an impressive backdrop as ex-Southern Railway 4-6-0 No 850 *Lord Nelson* accelerates the southbound 'Cumbrian Mountain Express' away from Appleby on 14 September 1983. *Tom Heavyside*

route continues to serve the public. Happily, much of the line's Victorian infrastructure remains intact, and it is possible, even in the 1980s, to visualise what the Settle & Carlisle railway must have looked like in its Edwardian heyday.

Departing from Leeds, present-day trains run northwestwards along the Little NWR line through Skipton and Hellifield, the route being shared by both Leeds-Morecambe and Leeds-Carlisle workings (see previous chapter). At Settle Junction the original Little NWR line diverges leftwards, and Carlisle trains turn northwards on to the 1876 Settle & Carlisle railway. With the A65 road running parallel first on the right and then on the left, trains continue northwards to Settle, the first intermediate station, and in many ways the southern 'terminus' of the Settle & Carlisle route.

Situated some 41 miles 33 chains from Leeds, Settle is a good example of one of the larger S&C stations. The main station building is on the up side, and like its counterparts at Kirkby Stephen and Appleby, this stone-built structure has two large and one smaller gable on the platform-facing side. A typical Settle & Carlisle type subsidiary waiting room remains intact on the down platform, and a standard Midland Railway signal cabin stands intact, though out of use, on the up side of the line.

From Settle the railway runs due north, with the River Ribble to the left and the B6479 road meandering from the left to the right-hand side of the line, and then back to the left once again. At Stainforth, the road deviates to the right for a second time, and this position is maintained for the next few miles.

Climbing steadily, trains eventually reach Horton-in-Ribblesdale, a classic Settle & Carlisle wayside station, with up and down platforms and standard, gabled buildings on the up side.

Northwards, the route continues through spectacular moorland scenery, and with the B6479 still running more or less parallel to the left, trains approach Ribblehead station and the mighty Ribblehead Viaduct. Ribblehead station (52 miles 13 chains) was used, for many years as a weather reporting post, and its stationmaster was required to take regular recordings of temperature, wind speed and humidity! Speeding through this isolated moorland station, northbound trains cross the B6255 road and are soon sweeping across the 24-span Ribblehead Viaduct, which is

Above:
In August 1965, an unidentified '9F' 2-10-0 heads a southbound freight towards Birkett Tunnel and Ais Gill summit.
W. J. V. Anderson

also known as Batty Moss Viaduct; below, countless humps and depressions in the surrounding moorland serve as curious reminders of the tramways and other temporary works used during the construction of the viaduct back in the 1870s.

Having crossed the majestic viaduct, trains thunder past the running loops and signalbox at Blea Moor; Blea Moor box is still open, but at night the isolation of this lonely box becomes only too apparent, and one reflects that the BR employees who man the mechanical box have much in common with their counterparts in the lighthouse service. In truth, Blea Moor signalbox can be a frightening place during the hours of darkness, when the relentless winds buffet its glass windows (and sometimes cause doors to fly suddenly and noisily open). On moonless nights the surrounding darkness is *total*, and the eerie atmosphere of

Below left:
The Settle & Carlisle as a diversionary route — Mark 3 stock indicates an Anglo-Scottish express, seen passing the village of Lazonby in the Eden Valley on 2 April 1983. *Tom Heavyside*

Below:
Emerging from Baron Wood Tunnel, Class 40 No 40074 heads a Perth-Manchester Red Bank empty van train towards the Pennines on 2 April 1983. *Tom Heavyside*

Blea Moor is magnified out of all proportion when telephones ring for no apparent reason — a result, it is said, of temperature changes having adverse effects upon the telephone lines.

Blea Moor Tunnel is situated immediately to the north of the box, and this 1½-mile bore also marks the boundary between Yorkshire and what is now Cumbria. Emerging into daylight once again, the railway soars across Dent Head Viaduct, and with lofty peaks such as Whernside (2,419ft) and Great Knoutberry Hill (2,203ft) visible on both sides of the line, the railway approaches Dent (58 miles 25 chains).

Built on a pronounced curve, Dent is one of the best known stations between Settle and Carlisle. Prior to rationalisation, its track layout had featured up and down refuge sidings, together with a small, single-siding goods yard on the down side. The main station building was also on the down side, and there was a small waiting room on the up platform; a standard Midland signal cabin remained in operation until the station ceased to be a block post at the end of January 1981.

From Dent, this heavily-engineered route continues towards its summit, and with spectacular scenery on all sides trains storm through Garsdale (61 miles 43 chains from Leeds). Once known as Hawes Junction & Garsdale, this remote outpost was formerly of some importance in that it was the junction for branch services to Hawes — at which place the Midland Railway made an end-on junction with the North Eastern trans-Pennine route from Northallerton. Three platforms were provided here, the up side being an island with tracks on either side, while the down side had just one platform face. Other facilities included a turntable, a water tower, an array of exchange sidings and station buildings which differed in relation to those found elsewhere on the Settle & Carlisle line.

From Garsdale, trains continue towards Ais Gill Summit, (1,167ft) and having surmounted this formidable obstacle, the route drops towards the pastoral Eden Valley. Kirkby Stephen, the next station (71 miles 40 chains) is similar to Settle, with 'large' Settle & Carlisle-type three-gable buildings and a large goods shed served by a loop siding; the modern BR signalbox is on the up side, and there was a characteristic Midland-type water tower at the southern end of the platform.

Above:
Vintage diesel power — a pair of Class 17 Bo-Bo diesel-electrics, working in multiple, pass the Midland Railway signalbox at Armathwaite with a trip freight in June 1968. *Peter W. Robinson*

Sweeping down towards the Eden Valley, northbound trains run through several closed stations, but Appleby (82 miles 15 chains) has remained an important stopping place for all services. Another of the 'large' S&C stations, Appleby has triple-gabled station buildings on the down platform, and a smaller waiting room on the up side. The up and down platforms are linked by a footbridge, and the goods sidings were concentrated on the down side, at the southern end of the passenger station.

Leaving Appleby, trains pass a succession of closed stations, one of which, at Culgaith, was notable in that it was unlike its counterparts elsewhere on the line. Significantly, this stopping place was opened on 1 April 1880 several months later than the other stations, and one assumes that the team of engineers and architects responsible for the Settle & Carlisle line had, by that time, been dispersed. This non-standard Settle & Carlisle station had a stone-built booking office and waiting room on the up side, and wooden waiting rooms on the down platform; the main building was not unlike Cromford, on the Matlock line. Unusually, a minor road crossed the line by means of a

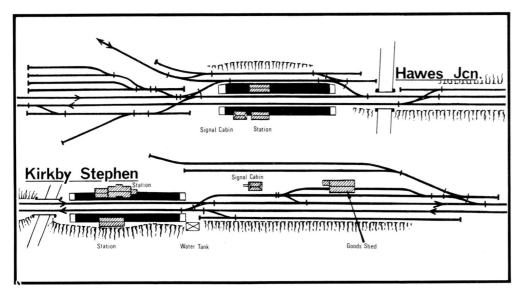

Left:
Trackplans: Hawes Junction (Garsdale) and Kirkby Stephen West, c1960.

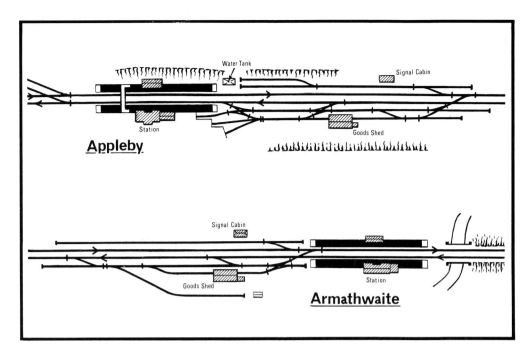

Appleby

Armathwaite

level crossing, while the goods yard had just one siding that was linked, by trailing crossovers, to both running lines.

It is often said that the northern sections of the Settle & Carlisle route are something of an anti-climax after the scenic splendours encountered further south, but this view is a gross over-simplification, and there is, in truth, much of interest between Appleby and Carlisle. The stations on this northern section are similar to those at Horton, Dent and elsewhere, but they are in many ways more attractive in that they are situated amidst much gentler scenery. Armathwaite (103 miles 2 chains from Leeds) was typical of the northern Settle & Carlisle stations. Situated in relatively well wooded surroundings, it had all the usual Settle & Carlisle features, including a twin-gabled building on the down side, a goods shed, cattle dock, and a standard Midland Railway signal cabin. Other characteristic MR features were much in evidence — notably the diagonal, slatted fencing which adorned both platforms.

Nearing Carlisle, the railway converges with the historic Newcastle & Carlisle line (see Chapter One) and trains then proceed over former NER metals into Carlisle Citadel station. Here, in a bustling, main line station on the rival West Coast route, the 113-mile scenic journey from Leeds comes to an end.

A Note on Train Services

Settle & Carlisle train services have undergone many fluctuations in recent years, but happily, there has been a gradual *increase* in terms of frequency since the withdrawal of stopping services in the 1960s. There were, at one time, just three up and three down trains on the entire line including the 'Thames-Clyde Express'; in May 1971 the first up train left Carlisle at 01.33, but this service was of no use to local travellers because it did not call at any of the intermediate stations between Carlisle and Skipton! The next up departure from Carlisle was the 'Thames-Clyde Express', which left at 12.19, and reached Skipton by 14.03, having called at both Appleby and Settle; finally, the 17.55

Above:
Having just left ex-LNER metals at Petteril Bridge Junction, 'Crab' Class 5MT 2-6-0 No 42831 heads south along the Settle & Carlisle with the 13.04 Carlisle-Skipton freight on 15 February 1964. *Peter J. Robinson*

express again called at Appleby and Settle, giving local residents a useful through service to Sheffield. In the reverse direction, there were trains from Skipton to Carlisle at 03.22, 10.03 and 14.11, and all of these InterCity workings served Settle and Appleby.

There have been two important developments since the 1970s, one welcome and the other perhaps less so; in 1982 the route lost its InterCity services and local travellers were left with a semi-fast service between Leeds and Carlisle. On the other hand, there has been a progressive reinstatement of stopping services and this development (initially designed to accommodate hikers and other tourists) has brought stopping services back to many of the smaller intermediate stations such as Dent and Ribblehead. At the same time, the Settle & Carlisle has found much favour as a steam route, with scheduled, steam-hauled excursions now a regular feature of the line's operation – a practise that will doubtless continue with the line's now-secure future.

CHAPTER FOUR

Coast to Coast; the CKP and the Stainmore Route

Jointly owned cross-country lines are particularly interesting to enthusiasts, and the Midland & Great Northern Joint Railway and (to a greater extent) the Somerset & Dorset Joint Railway have enjoyed ample coverage in the railway press; less well known, perhaps, is the former Cockermouth, Keswick & Penrith (CKP) line, which once ran from east to west through the Cumbrian mountains, giving enthusiasts the chance to ride on an English mountain railway every bit as spectacular as its counterparts in Scotland and Wales.

History of the Cockermouth Keswick & Penrith Railway

The Cockermouth, Keswick & Penrith was built as a link between the Cumbrian coast ironworks and the Durham coalfield, so that good quality Durham coke could be used in Cumberland furnaces — the local coal being unsuitable for that purpose. The scheme's promoters included both landowners and industrialists, and those associated with the project included Sir Henry Ralph Vane of Penrith; Reginald Dykes Marshall of Leeds; John Steel MP, of Cockermouth; John Harris of Workington; Henry Pease of

Darlington, and T. Hoskins of Cockermouth. The CKP prospectus spoke enthusiastically of a 'large traffic in haematite ore from mines near Whitehaven', together with 'local traffic in coal, lime and passengers'.

Confident that their ore-carrying railway was destined for early and spectacular success, the promoters obtained an Act for construction of 'a railway from Cockermouth to Keswick and Penrith'. The Act (24 & 25 Vic. cap 203) was dated 1 August 1861, and it defined the proposed line as:

'A railway commencing by a junction with the Cockermouth and Workington Railway at a point distant six hundred and forty yards or thereabouts, westwards of the passenger station of that railway, in the township of Brigham, and thence passing from, in, through or into the parishes, townships and extra-parochial places following; or some of them, that is to say, Brigham, Cockermouth, Embleton, Setmurthy, Wythop, Above Derwent, Underskiddaw, Keswick, Saint John's Castle-rigg and Wythburn, Greta Mills and Briery Cottages, Threlkeld, Mungrisdale, Hutton Soil, Hutton John, Newbiggin, Stainton and Penrith, and terminating in a field called Miresbeck Field, otherwise New Lands Close, at or near Newlands Terrace, in the parish of Penrith, all in the county of Cumberland.'

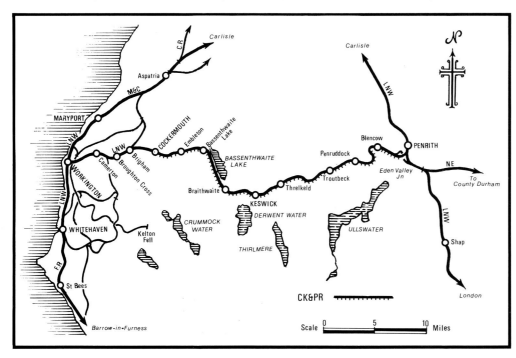

Left:
The Cockermouth Keswick & Penrith Railway, 1923.

There would be, in addition to the main line, a short branch to the Lancaster & Carlisle Railway at Penrith, and the Act made careful provision for this important section of line which was defined as:

'A branch railway, wholly situate in the parish of Penrith, commencing by a junction with the Lancaster and Carlisle Railway, at a point distant about six hundred and fifteen yards southwards of the passenger station of the last-mentioned railway, and not at any other point without the consent in writing of the Lancaster and Carlisle Railway Company, and terminating by a junction with the main line before described, in a field called Mains, in the occupation of Joseph Fenton, at a point distant about one hundred and thirty yards southwest of the junction of the branch railway with the Lancaster and Carlisle Railway.'

Having obtained their Act, the CKP promoters lost little time in implementing their scheme, and at the half-year meeting held in 1862 the delighted shareholders learned that the works would commence 'as soon as the directors are in a position to proceed with them'. *The Railway Times* commented that the new railway would provide 'railway accommodation in a locality much in need of it', while at the same time the completed line would 'bring the east and west coasts of the iron-producing districts into direct communication with each other'.

The 31-mile-long CKP route was opened for goods and mineral traffic on 1 November 1864, and to passengers on 2 January 1865 (after the raw new embankments had been consolidated by the passage of heavy ore trains). Although the Cockermouth, Keswick & Penrith was an independent company with its own board of directors, it had no locomotives or rolling stock of its own, and for this reason the line was worked jointly by the London & North Western and North Eastern companies. The LNWR provided passenger services, while the North Eastern worked the heavy mineral trains which ran westwards from

County Durham via the South Durham & Lancashire Union Railway of 1861, and thence along the Eden Valley route to Penrith.

With the decline of the local iron industry from the 1890s onwards, tourist traffic became increasingly important, and in its later years the route boasted its very own named train – the 'Lakes Express' – which conveyed through coaches from London to Workington. There was, on the other hand, little attempt to run through passenger services from the Northeast, though the NER took advantage of its running powers in 1911, and introduced a short-lived summer service from Darlington to Keswick; this ceased in 1914 but a seasonal, Sundays-only Newcastle train ran in later years.

By 1938 the LMS (which absorbed the CKP in 1923) was providing a basic passenger service of about nine trains each way. On the freight side, traffic remained heavy until the relative decline of the West Cumberland industrial areas after World War 1, and thereafter cross-country mineral trains ceased to use the CKP, which became primarily a holiday route.

The line was, by this time, notable in that it continued to be worked by archaic locomotives such as the 'Jumbo' 2-4-0s and 'Cauliflower' 0-6-0s which became so much a feature of the route. Indeed, the last-named locomotives

Above:
Overgrown trackwork emphasises impending closure as Class 3MT 2-6-0 No 77002 and Class 4MT No 76074 breast Stainmore summit with a Newcastle-Blackpool train.
The late Derek Cross

Left:
Still over 1,000ft above sea level, two Ivatt Class 4MT 2-6-0s descend towards Belah with a westbound summer Saturday holiday working, bound for Blackpool.
The late Derek Cross

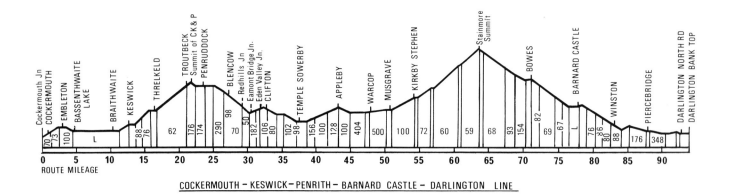

remained at work on the line until the 1950s, when a programme of underline bridge renewals allowed more modern motive power, including Ivatt 2-6-0s, to work over this spectacular route. In 1955, Derby Lightweight multiple-units were introduced on local workings, but Ivatt 2-6-0s continued to work the 'Lakes Express', with No 46432 being a regular performer; other regulars included Nos 46426, 46458 and 46488.

Along the Line from Penrith to Cockermouth

In its heyday, the Cockermouth, Keswick & Penrith line provided a fascinating way to see large areas of Northern Lakeland. Passenger services ran to and from Penrith, on the WCML, where CKP trains used the westernmost of the station's three platforms. Leaving Penrith, trains ran

Above:
Gradient Profile: Cockermouth to Darlington.

alongside the main line before diverging westwards on to the CKP proper. A direct line converged from the right at Redhills Junction where a burrowing junction from the LNWR enabled NER mineral trains to avoid Penrith; this connection was lifted in the 1930s following the demise of Durham-Cumberland cross-country traffic.

Hurrying away from the busy main line, CKP trains climbed into a rather bleak, desolate region on gradients as steep as 1 in 70; this eastern section was, until 1936, double-

Below:
Some sample CKP trackplans of the 1950s. Note that, in each case, long running loops were provided for mineral traffic. Threlkeld's layout was made more complex by the provision of quarry sidings, while Cockermouth was notable in that its extensive goods sidings were also used to stable coaching stock.

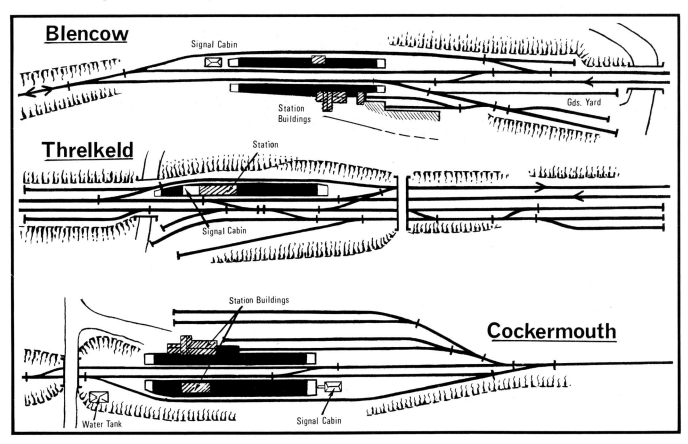

tracked from Redhills Junction as far as the first intermediate station at Blencow, some 3¾ miles from Penrith. Up and down platforms were provided here, with solid Jacobean-style stone buildings on the down side. The rather cramped goods yard was also on the down side, and included a loading bank, cattle dock and coal drops, but no goods shed. A long goods loop bypassed the platforms on the up side, recalling the days when sturdy NER 0-6-0s struggled to haul their long mineral trains over this difficult mountain route.

From Blencow, the CKP followed a serpentine course up into the Cumbrian mountains in an attempt to find the easiest route; even so, the exhaust beats of the labouring engines left no doubt that the overall direction was upwards! The view from the carriage windows was one of complete desolation, with lonely hills stretching away on both sides and the rounded tops of Mell Fell (1,760ft) and Little Mell Fell (1,657ft) providing the only visual interest in an otherwise dreary moorland landscape. In former times, this remote, backward region witnessed tragedies of famine and starvation, notably during the early 17th century when the parish registers of nearby Greystoke recorded the deaths of 'a poor fellow destitute of succour', 'a poor hungerstarved beggar', and 'a poor beggar stripling born upon the borders of England'.

Still climbing, the trains reached double track again at Penruddock, a small station on the very edge of the Lake District National Park. Beyond, the line continued to its remote, windswept summit near Troutbeck station (10 miles). Situated almost 900ft above sea level, this isolated station had only an inn and post office for company! Westwards, the double-track line descended towards Threlkeld (14¾ miles from Penrith), at which point the line became single for the remainder of the way to Cockermouth.

Threlkeld had an unusual island layout, with extensive stone station buildings incorporating a signalbox at one end; pedestrian access was via a low-level entrance and connecting subway. Lengthy goods sidings extended eastwards on the down side to serve the important Threlkeld micro-granite quarries which had provided stone for the construction of the CKP. At their peak, the quarries produced up to 80,000 tons of granite a year — much of this tonnage being transported by rail. In the 1890s, the installation of a precast concrete plant enabled the quarry to supply concrete flagstones for many Lancashire industrial towns.

From Threlkeld, the railway followed the picturesque Greta Valley for about two miles, crossing the river several times and passing through the short Greta Tunnel before reaching the important intermediate station at Keswick (18¼ miles).

Keswick had three platform faces, with extensive 'Seaside Swiss' chalet-style buildings on the up side and solid, rather gloomy stone buildings (which were perhaps more typical of Lake District railway architecture) on the down platform. Nearby, the four-storey Keswick Hotel, built by the CKP in 1869, demonstrated the company's very real commitment to tourism and underlined the close links between railways and the Victorian holiday industry. These links were of particular importance to Keswick, which had been in a state of decline prior to the opening of the CKP; by the late 1880s, however, up to 50,000 holidaymakers

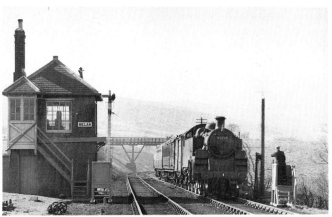

Top:
The South Durham & Lancashire Union Railway was opened in 1861, three years before the CKP: its most famous engineering feature was the Belah Viaduct, designed by Thomas Bouch of Tay Bridge notoriety. This 1960 view shows a Penrith to Darlington local train heading eastwards across the viaduct. *The late Derek Cross*

Above:
The Belah signalman collects the token from the driver of Class 3MT 2-6-2T No 82028 as it heads towards Stainmore summit with the 10.32 Penrith-Darlington train, on 10 March 1956. As the track was double at this location, the use of a single-line token suggests temporary engineering works. *J. W. Armstrong*

were visiting the town each year, and Keswick was firmly established as a rather 'select' Lakeland resort.

Continuing westwards, trains crossed the pastoral Vale of Keswick — a low-lying tract of land stretching from Derwentwater to Bassenthwaite Lake. Braithwaite, the next stop, was a small single platform station situated in pleasant, well-wooded surroundings. Beyond, the single line turned northwards to gain the western shore of Bassenthwaite Lake. Trains followed the shore line for the next four miles, giving travellers many fine views through the window of lofty Skiddaw (3,054ft) on the far side of the lake.

Bassenthwaite Lake station was situated on the very shores of the lake, and had a very long passing loop, divided into two by an intermediate crossover (presumably to increase line capacity when freight traffic was still of some importance to the route). The main station buildings, on the down side, were simple though not unattractive stone structures, and the up platform boasted a small wooden waiting room; unusually, this station also functioned as a rural post office! A four-road goods yard was located on the up side, though there was little originating traffic apart from occasional shipments of timber.

Having reached the northern end of the lake, trains turned westwards once more, and, climbing at 1 in 100, reached Embleton, the penultimate station. This was, like Braithwaite, a small, single-platform affair, with a refuge siding in lieu of a passing loop. Beyond, the single-track route dropped towards Cockermouth on a 1 in 74 gradient.

Situated just outside the National Park, the town of Cockermouth was much visited by tourists wishing to see William Wordsworth's birthplace in the High Street. The station was similar to others en route from Penrith, and had up and down platforms with an additional goods loop on the down side, giving three through roads in all. There was a small goods yard on the up side, where several dead-end sidings fanned outwards to serve coal wharves and a cattle dock. The stone station buildings incorporated a stationmaster's house, together with the usual booking offices and waiting room.

Although Cockermouth was the western extremity of the CKP, it was not the end of the line, as the route continued, as a purely LNWR line, to Workington and the Cumbrian coast industrial areas that had given birth to the railway back in the 1860s.

In common with other holiday lines, the CKP carried a heavy traffic during the summer months, but very little at other times of the year; packed trains in July and August could not support the railway throughout the year, and by 1961 the local DMU service was reputed to be losing £1,000 per week. The Beeching era ended with the inevitable closures, and the line was closed to all traffic west of

Keswick on 16 April 1966, ultimately leaving the Keswick to Penrith section as a long siding working from Penrith as a dead-end branch. Goods yards were closed, passing loops lifted, and stations were reduced to unstaffed halts.

By 1967, the double-tracked Penruddock to Threlkeld section had been taken out of use, while Keswick itself became an unstaffed halt in July 1968. Many of these measures were false economies. With no run-round loop at Keswick, for example, it became difficult to run excursions, and a useful source of additional traffic was thrown away. Not surprisingly traffic declined still further, and the line was closed from Monday 6 March 1972.

As there was no Sunday service, the last trains ran on Saturday 4 March, amid desolate snowstorms which added further misery to an already sombre occasion. The scene was completed by a 'Victorian mourning party' from Lancaster University, who wore black top hats and frock coats as a satirical comment on BR's decision to let the railway die.

The very last train was an eight-car DMU special, chartered by Keswick Round Table and timetabled to leave Keswick at 22.05 on Saturday evening. Some 450 people made this sad, final journey through the night, while others watched silently from the lineside as 108 years of railway history drew to a close. The line was lifted shortly after, and many sections of the route have since been made into roads.

In retrospect, the closure of the CKP in its original form was inevitable; the line had been built to serve particular industries, and when those industries went into decline there was no reason to keep the railway open. Viewed in this light, it is surprising that the Workington to Penrith route (and its eastern continuation to County Durham) survived as long as it did. On the other hand, there were sound reasons for retaining the Penrith to Keswick section, which, as a branch of the electrified WCML could perhaps

Right:
A deceptive air of 'mainline' normality characterises this shot of Class 4MT 2-6-0 No 43120 shunting the exchange sidings at Merrygill quarry, east of Kirkby Stephen, on 12 June 1967. With the ending of this traffic, and the closure of Kirkby Stephen East coal sidings, in 1972, this surviving stub of the Stainmore route was cut back to Warcop Army depot.
John R. P. Hunt

have found a niche in the modern transport system. One wonders, in fact, what might have happened had the Keswick line survived another two years; would BR have closed it *after* the oil crisis? Perhaps not, and one has only to look at the present high loadings on the neighbouring Windermere branch to see what modest development might have done for the popular Keswick line.

The Stainmore Route

As mentioned earlier, the Cockermouth Keswick & Penrith Railway could not have existed in isolation, and although the company was an independent concern the CKP's Victorian promoters saw their railway as a continuation of an existing east-to-west traffic artery from County Durham.

It would be useful therefore to examine the easternmost section of line between Penrith and Darlington – the spectacular Stainmore route which brought the North Eastern Railway over the Pennines and into contact with its allies at Penrith.

Origins of the Stainmore Route

The North Eastern Railway has, arguably, received little attention from writers or historians – which is surprising when one remembers that this important, regionally-based company was (by amalgamation) a lineal descendant of the pioneering Stockton & Darlington Railway (S&DR) – the world's first public steam railway.

The story of the Stockton & Darlington is too well known to need recounting in detail; the company was formed in 1821, when an Act was obtained to construct a railway from Stockton-on-Tees to Witton Park colliery, near Shildon. The first train ran on 27 September 1825 and although passenger trains were initially horse-drawn, the S&DR was the first steam-operated public railway in the world.

The S&DR commenced regular steam-hauled passenger services in 1833, and in the next few years the original short section of line was gradually extended; Bishop Auckland, for example, was reached in 1843, while in 1856 the route was further extended to serve Barnard Castle.

Ambitious entrepreneurs – many of them Quakers – were soon planning a variety of additional lines, one of which was the South Durham & Lancashire Union Railway. Designed from its inception as a cross-country mineral line, this Stockton & Darlington-backed scheme sought to link Bishop Auckland and Tebay in order that Durham coke could be easily transported to the ironworks of Furness. Engineered by Thomas Bouch, the railway was opened for freight traffic on 4 July 1861 and for passengers on 8 August; its route was spectacular, with fearsome gradients on either side of Stainmore summit and an immense lattice girder viaduct at Belah, to the east of Kirkby Stephen.

Meanwhile, in 1858, an Act (21 & 22 Vic. cap 14) had been obtained for construction of the Eden Valley Railway between Kirkby Stephen and Penrith, and when opened (for minerals on 10 April and for passengers on 7 June 1862) the new railway was taken over by the Stockton & Darlington company; in the following year the S&DR was itself absorbed by the North Eastern Railway and the Darlington to Penrith line thereby became an appendage of the NER.

Locomotive Notes

The completed Stainmore line was soon carrying significant quantities of coke, and in view of the arduous nature of this trans-Pennine route the Stockton & Darlington introduced a series of powerful 0-6-0 mineral engines with 5ft wheels and 17in×24in inside cylinders; known as the '1001' class these long-lived locomotives were, in effect, the culmination of many years' development of the Stephenson long-boiler type. Another class designed primarily for work on the Stainmore line were Wordsell's famous 'T' class 0-8-0s, the first of which appeared in 1901.

Passenger trains were originally hauled by 4-4-0s such as the S&DR locomotives *Brougham* and *Lowther*; these two engines were provided with commodious cabs, but local enginemen apparently preferred *open* footplates, and subsequent S&DR 4-4-0s such as *Keswick* (1862) were

cabless. Fletcher '901' class 2-4-0s worked on the Stainmore route for many years, and in 1936 ex-Great Eastern Railway 'E4' 2-4-0s were transferred to the North Eastern area for work on the Tebay line and elsewhere; the engines involved were in BR days Nos 62781, 62784, 62788, 62793, 62795 and 62797. Later, around 1951, many services were worked by ex-NER 'J21' class 0-6-0s – the GER engines having been returned to East Anglia in 1941-42. Modern types seen on the line included Ivatt Moguls and BR Standard classes.

The Route Described

Stainmore route trains commenced their trans-Pennine journeys at Darlington Bank Top, where a large, triple-section overall roof served as an imposing monument to Victorian engineering skills. Leaving the station, trains followed the East Coast main line for a short distance before diverging leftwards to join the original Stockton & Darlington route. With large-scale industry visible on all sides, the line continued towards Darlington North Road.

Situated just 1 mile 23 chains from Bank Top, North Road was an exceptionally early station that had been opened in 1842 as a replacement for an even earlier station; an elegant, though somewhat severe structure, its main facade incorporated a two-storey central block with flanking single-storey pavilions. The high-level platforms were covered by a wooden train shed, while the main entrance featured a projecting colonade with slender cast iron columns.

Heading due west, Penrith trains left the Stockton & Darlington route at Hopetown Junction, and then continued along the Tees Valley via Piercebridge and Gainford. Running through pleasant, agricultural country-side, this first section of line was easily-graded, but climbing commenced in earnest beyond Gainford station (8 miles 78 chains), the steepest gradients being 1 in 74. The intermediate stations at Piercebridge, Gainford and Winston were broadly similar, with the same low-roofed, brick-built station buildings; Piercebridge and Winston had glazed waiting areas fronting the platforms, but at Gainford the recessed centre section formed an open loggia.

Continuing westwards, trains soon reached Barnard Castle (16 miles 57 chains from Bank Top). The station here was of typical S&DR design, with a single through platform for up and down passenger traffic and a number of goods loops, by means of which heavy mineral trains were able to bypass the passenger station; there were terminal bays at each end of the main platform, and a miniature overall roof provided a modicum of protection for waiting travellers.

Running now on the former South Durham & Lancashire Union line, trains climbed through an area of wild, inhospitable moorland on gradients as steep as 1 in 70. The 13-mile ascent towards Stainmore Summit featured a large number of impressive viaducts, some of which were constructed of local stone while others were of metal; the 740ft-long Deepdale Viaduct, for instance, was a classic Bouch-type girder structure, with slender struts and columns that seemed, at first glance, to be incapable of supporting a train. These unusual metal viaducts were similar to Thomas Bouch's ill-fated Tay Bridge – though in fairness to this much-maligned Victorian engineer, it should be stressed that Deepdale Viaduct stood firm for many years!

With the A66 running parallel on the right, the route reached its summit at Stainmore. Set in a bleak depression, the actual summit was 30 miles 25 chains from Darlington, and some 1,370ft above mean sea level; no station was provided, but the summit was marked by the presence of a large metal elevation sign, together with up and down running loops and a standard NER signal cabin. The brick-built box was, unusually, rendered – probably to give added protection from the vehement winter weather experienced in this remote and inhospitable place.

Having surmounted its summit (the second highest in England), the route dropped towards Kirkby Stephen on a succession of favourable gradients, which included 2½ miles at 1 in 59, 3½ miles at 1 in 60 and 2 miles at 1 in 72. Nearing Barras station, the line curved southwestwards in a huge arc as it attempted to find an easy descent, but this serpentine course meant that the railway crossed several deep defiles at right angles, and this in turn, necessitated several more bridges and viaducts – including the famous Belah Viaduct between Barras and Kirkby Stephen.

In common with many other bridges designed by Thomas Bouch, the Belah Viaduct represented an attempt to combine strength with lightweight construction, and to achieve this laudable aim the engineer chose a system of lattice piers, each of which utilised six vertical iron columns, together with a series of interlinked struts and braces; these lightweight piers supported the main horizontal girders, which were again of lattice construction, with catwalks along each side. The resulting structure was 1,040ft long and, at its highest point, approximately 200ft above the valley floor. In retrospect, these Bouch-designed viaducts were compromised by the use of iron rather than steel components, and in this sense they were probably ahead of their time; nevertheless, the Belah Viaduct carried trains of far greater weight than those envisaged by Thomas Bouch, and to that extent the bridge (and its much-maligned designer) could be described as a success.

Still heading in a southwesterly direction, the route continued to Kirkby Stephen (39 miles 54 chains), an important intermediate station with extensive buildings and an overall roof. The passenger station was flanked, on its south side, by a series of goods loops, and to the north, by the goods yard, cattle docks and locomotive depot. The line divided into two at the west end of the station, with one line heading due west towards Tebay while the other diverged north along the Eden Valley.

Taking the Eden Valley route, Penrith-bound trains entered an area noted for its dairy produce, and with attractive, pastoral scenery visible on each side of the line, trains soon reached Musgrave – where the River Eden was spanned by a viaduct of stone and iron.

Warcop, the next stop, was similar to other stations on the Eden Valley line, with a single platform and substantial station buildings; the main block was a single-storey gabled structure with a projecting bay window, and a two-storey cross-wing provided domestic accommodation for the stationmaster and his family. The small, rectangular signalbox was a single-storey building on the end of the platform; nearby, an army training camp provided an additional source of traffic at this otherwise remote place, and large troop movements could, on occasions, bring nine or 10-coach military specials to this part of the route.

Continuing westwards, trains reached Appleby (50 miles 63 chains). The loop here was more than ½ mile long, but only one platform was provided for passenger traffic. The station house and adjacent offices presented a handsome appearance, being constructed of local red sandstone; built in a rustic style, they featured overhanging gables and steeply-pitched roofs. To the left, a double-track spur provided a useful link to the neighbouring Settle & Carlisle line, which was used not only by freight trains, but (from 1880 until 1893) by timetabled MR passenger services between Appleby (Midland) and Penrith via the Eden Valley line.

From Appleby, the line passed beneath the Midland route and then fell towards Kirkby Thore on gradients of 1 in 100 and 1 in 155; like Warcop, Kirkby Thore was another small station serving a predominantly rural community.

Curving on to a westerly alignment, the single-track railway headed towards its junction with the LNWR main

Top:
Weight restrictions meant that certain ex-LNWR classes worked on the CKP for many years, more modern locomotives being too heavy for some bridges. This August 1936 view shows two 'Cauliflower' 0-6-0s, Nos 8580 and 8544, departing from Keswick with a heavy eastbound train. *H. N. James*

Above:
On 2 April 1966, only two weeks before closure west of Keswick, immaculate Ivatt Class 2MTs Nos 46458 and 46426 prepare to leave Keswick with the 'Lakes & Fells Railtour'. The Keswick hotel can be seen behind the leading locomotive.
The late Derek Cross

line and, falling steadily, the route reached its lowest point near the wayside station at Temple Sowerby. Of similar appearance to Warcop and other Eden Valley stations, this small stopping place had just one platform, and its attractive buildings exhibited an air of rustic *gemütlich*; to paraphrase C. Hamilton Ellis, one felt that this NER station should have been called *Something Cottage* – and perhaps be sited in the Home Counties instead of the Northern Fells! Of stone, timber and timber-frame construction, the building was replete with gables, finials, and a profusion of ornate tudor-style chimneys. A projecting bay window was again provided, although this particular feature was more than mere decoration in that, in earlier days, it would probably have housed the telegraph instruments.

Beyond Temple Sowerby, the line climbed towards Eden Valley Junction, at which point the Stainmore route

converged with the former LNWR main line; when first opened, the junction had faced southwards, but this configuration was hardly convenient for coast-to-coast mineral traffic, and on 7 July 1862 the S&DR (which had by that time assumed control of the Eden Valley Railway) obtained Parliamentary consent for a deviation towards Penrith. When opened in August 1863 this new, north-facing curve, provided a better path for through freight trains, and enabled trains from the Stainmore route to reach the LNWR station at Penrith without reversing.

Gaining the WCML, trains continued northwestwards passed the link to the Cockermouth Keswick & Penrith line at Eamount Bridge Junction, and finally drew to a stand in Penrith station, where the 64 mile 75 chain journey from Darlington came to an end.

Although the cross-country mineral traffic for which the CKP and Stainmore routes had been built evaporated after World War 1, reduced numbers of freight trains continued to use the Stainmore route in order to reach the Furness area. The Stainmore route was always a difficult one to work, the problem of severe gradients being compounded by weight-restricted viaducts; passenger services were dieselised in January 1958, but had dwindled to only three each way by the early 1960s. Meanwhile, BR was evaluating alternative routes for surviving east-west freight traffic, and the railway was closed in January 1962, apart from the Darlington to Barnard Castle service which lasted for a further two years.

Above left:
Dieselisation came early to the CKP, but although travellers were said to appreciate the views from the new DMUs, financial losses continued. Snow lies on Skiddaw (3,054ft) as a Derby Lightweight DMU enters Keswick on 2 April 1966.
The late Derek Cross

Above:
Deserted platforms at Cockermouth witness the departure of the Workington portion of the up 'Lakes Express' on 20 August 1964. *The late Derek Cross*

Happily, the western end of the route survived, at least in part, as a freight-only branch from Appleby, the reason for this unexpected survival being the army camp at Warcop. For a time, the line also carried aggregates from Merrygill quarry, but on 3 November 1975 Warcop became the end of the line. In the early 1980s, there were from two to three goods trains each week between Appleby and Warcop, together with sporadic troop specials. Motive power seen in recent years included Class 25s, Class 40s and Class 47s.

In March 1989, BR announced the closure of the Warcop branch, despite its popularity with railtour operators and (unconfirmed) reports that the MoD staff would have preferred its retention. Reprieve of the S&C main line one month later was not accompanied by a similar reprieve for the branch, though, at the time of writing a consortium was considering leasing the branch for preserved steam operation.

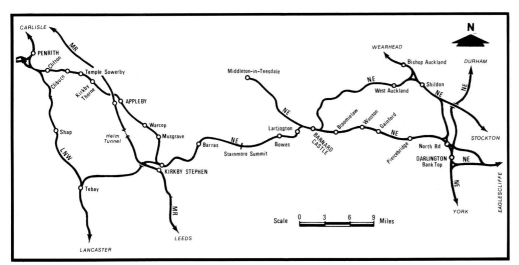

Left:
The Stainmore route, showing pre-Grouping ownership.

CHAPTER FIVE

Two Lancashire & Yorkshire Routes

A small but busy system of some 600 route miles, the Lancashire & Yorkshire Railway (L&Y) was a Pennine railway *par excellence*, being confined, in the main, to the hilly, industrial areas of Lancashire and the West Riding of Yorkshire. There were, it is true, several lines in the flat, pastoral lowlands of the Fylde, but otherwise the L&Y traversed a landscape of wild moorlands and great industrial towns — the very heartland of the industrial revolution. It follows that most L&Y routes were 'Pennine routes', but lack of space precludes adequate coverage of the entire system; instead, it is proposed to concentrate in this chapter on two classic trans-Pennine cross-country lines — the existing Preston to Colne branch and the now-closed Manchester to Hellifield route which crossed the Preston-Colne line at Blackburn.

The Historical Setting

Railway history is, at the best of times, a complex story of conflicting aims and ambitions played out by rival groups of promoters, and nowhere is this axiom more apparent than in the narrow, upland valleys of East Lancashire. The primary power source of the 18th century Industrial Revolution had been water, and by the 1840s towns such as Blackburn, Burnley and Bolton had spread themselves out along convenient valley bottoms, with textile mills dotted at regular intervals along the fast-flowing moorland streams. These mills were symbols of growing and prosperous communities, and despite the overcrowding and regimentation of industrialisation, country dwellers continued to migrate towards the new towns. Population figures reflect this new-found prosperity; Bolton, for instance, had grown from a town of 17,416 people in 1801 to a bustling mill town with 41,195 inhabitants by 1831. Neighbouring Blackburn had, similarly, increased its population from 11,980 in 1801 to 27,091 by the early 1830s.

Contemporary writers and travellers were impressed by the size of these new towns, and by the scale and efficiency of their industries. Indeed, as early as 1795, J. Aikin had noted how 'the invention and improvements of machines' had extended trade and 'called in hands from all parts' to work in the mills. At Bury, for example, cotton manufacture was carried on very extensively:

'A great number of factories are erected upon the rivers and upon many brooks within the parish, for carding and

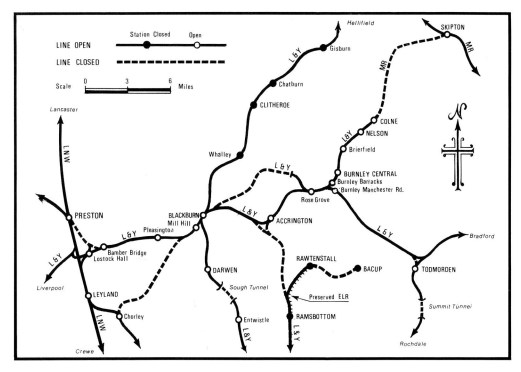

Left:
East Lancashire Railways in the 1980s. Note that the Blackburn-Hellified line is used as a diversionary route although it is officially closed to passengers.

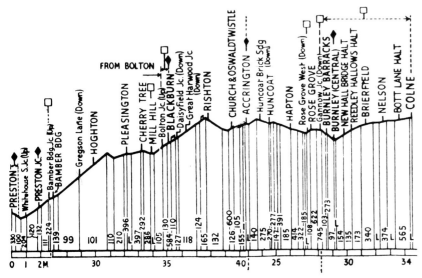
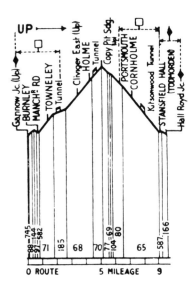

spinning both cotton and sheep's wool, also for fulling woollen cloth. The inventions and improvements here in different branches are astonishing.'

The story was repeated at Blackburn which, according to Aikin, had 'long been known as a manufacturing place', and at Darwen where a small village had become 'a populous district manufacturing a large quantity of cotton goods'.

The Blackburn & Preston Railway

Towns such as Bury and Blackburn did not feature in many of the early railway schemes, and having been bypassed by the Preston & Lancaster, North Union and other main line routes, the inhabitants of these isolated places were understandably keen that their growing townships should be linked to the new railway system. There were, as a result, several locally-based railway projects which, in the 1840s, sought to bring rail transport to the mill towns of East Lancashire. The Blackburn & Preston Railway was typical of these small companies; formed by an Act of 6 June 1844 (7 & 8 Vic. cap 34) the company was empowered to make a branch 'from the town of Blackburn to the North Union Railway, in the township of Farrington near Preston, in the county of Lancaster'. The authorised route traversed easy terrain, and this modest local line was opened to traffic on 1 June 1846.

The Manchester Bury & Rawtenstall Railway

Meanwhile, further south, the Manchester Bury & Rawtenstall Railway had been formed to construct a line between Manchester and a string of towns to the north of that city. The Rawtenstall promoters obtained their Act on 4 July 1844 (7 & 8 Vic. cap 60), and with an authorised capital of £300,000 the Manchester Bury & Rawtenstall seemed destined for success. Commencing by a junction with the Manchester & Bolton Railway at Clifton, the line headed northwards to Bury, passing en route through an important mining area that was expected to yield substantial revenues from mineral traffic; from Bury, the authorised route continued northwards, via Ramsbottom and Stubbins, to its terminus at Rawtenstall. Construction presented many problems, and the works included numerous cuttings, embankments, and a tunnel at Summerseat.

Above:
Gradient Profiles: Preston to Colne line and Burnley to Todmorden line. *From* **Gradient Profiles M37, M39 & M40**

Below:
Under the control of Preston power signalling centre, Class 47 No 47432 emerges from Blackburn Tunnel and takes the Hellifield line at Daisyfield Junction with a diverted down express on 2 April 1988. *Les Nixon*

Bottom:
Steam survived until 1968 in East Lancashire. In April 1966, an '8F' 2-8-0 No 48730 takes the Padiham line at Rose Grove with a coal train for the nearby power station. Rose Grove depot's coaling stage can be seen above the locomotive's tender. *Les Nixon*

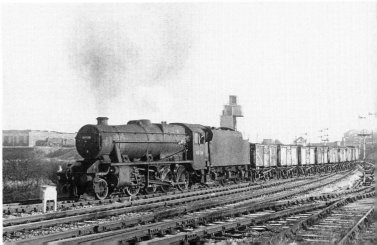

The Blackburn Burnley Accrington & Colne Extension Railway

There was as yet no physical connection between the Manchester Bury & Rawtenstall Railway and the nearby Blackburn & Preston line, but in the early months of 1845 a further Bill was sent up to Parliament with the aim of seeking consent for an extension of the Rawtenstall route 'to the towns of Blackburn, Burnley, Accrington and Colne'. The Bill was presented on 10 February 1845, accompanied by petitions from 'the owners and occupiers of property and inhabitants on the line or in the neighbourhood of the proposed railway'. Further petitions were received from the towns of Accrington, Haslingden, Colne, Clitheroe and Skipton, and with solid local support the Blackburn Burnley Accrington & Colne Extension Railway had little difficulty in obtaining its Royal Assent on 30 June 1845.

Formation of the East Lancashire Railway

Having obtained their Act, the line's supporters lost no time in amalgamating their undertaking with the still-unfinished Manchester Bury & Rawtenstall Railway. This was, to say the least, a questionable stratagem because Rawtenstall shares were worth £17 each at the time of amalgamation whereas Blackburn Burnley Accrington & Colne shares were worth only £6 10s! Nevertheless, the merger went ahead as planned and the two companies were reborn as the East Lancashire Railway (ELR); these arrangements were formalised by an Act of 3 August 1846 (9 & 10 Vic. cap 302) which constituted the ELR with a capital of £1,020,000 in shares and powers to raise a further £296,000 by loan.

The newly-created East Lancashire Railway was born in a period of acute economic crisis, but at a time when many other companies were unable to complete their authorised schemes the ELR was able to forge ahead with work on the Rawtenstall line, which was opened, with much rejoicing, on 28 September 1846.

Work on the Accrington extension was, by this time, well under way, and on 17 August 1848 this last-named line was opened through to Accrington. The railway reached Burnley on 1 December 1848, and was completed throughout to Colne on 1 February 1849; at Colne the line formed a connection with an extension of the Midland Railway from Skipton.

The East Lancashire Railway was, unfortunately, soon involved in a dispute with the Lancashire & Yorkshire Railway (which had absorbed the Manchester & Bolton line). The ELR was legally bound to pay tolls for use of the section of line between Clifton Junction and Manchester, and for the first few months of operation the East Lancashire had run some trains through to Manchester without stopping — afterwards making a declaration for toll purposes of the number of passengers carried aboard each train. Distrusting the ELR to furnish accurate figures, the L&Y decided that *all* trains would be stopped at Clifton so that passengers could be counted, and perhaps inevitably, the East Lancashire objected most strongly to this insulting action. The scene was thus set for the 'Battle of Clifton Junction' which took place on 12 March 1849 after the Lancashire & Yorkshire had blocked the line at Clifton. The result was a somewhat farcical pushing competition between an up ELR working and an opposing L&Y train. Thereafter, the situation rapidly escalated into a general confrontation, and although a large body of policemen prevented physical violence, there was total disruption of services, with (at one stage) no less than eight trains held up on both companies' lines.

The problems at Clifton Junction could not be satisfactorily resolved, and following this major confrontation, East Lancashire trains ceased running into Manchester Victoria. In the meantime, the warring companies became involved in further clashes at Blackburn where, in 1850, the ELR tried to extract exorbitant tolls from the Lancashire & Yorkshire company. Before describing the 'Battle of Blackburn' it would, however, be useful to go back four years in order to look in detail at the Blackburn Clitheroe & North Western Junction Railway — the second Lancashire & Yorkshire route to be described in this present chapter.

Origins of the Clitheroe Line

The Clitheroe line was, like its counterparts elsewhere in the Lancashire industrial region, an essentially local scheme, which had been formed to bring railway communication to a group of hitherto isolated textile-producing towns. The proposed line was on the periphery of

Top:
On 2 April 1988, a northbound express, headed by Class 47 No 47645 *Robert F. Fairlie* and diverted via the Ribble Valley line, pulls out of Blackburn. *Les Nixon*

Above:
Intermediate stations between Blackburn and Hellifield were closed in 1962. Here, Class 50 No 50031 (later named *Hood*) passes the abandoned platforms at Wilpshire with a diverted Manchester — Glasgow express. *Tom Heavyside*

Lancashire's industrial heartlands, and in addition to serving small manufacturing towns such as Whalley and Clitheroe, the Blackburn Clitheroe & North Western Junction Railway would also serve a prosperous agricultural area that was expected to benefit from the opening-up of new markets in nearby urban centres.

The Clitheroe line originated in 1846 when a group of local entrepreneurs approached Parliament with a Bill 'for making a railway with branches therefrom, in the County of Lancaster, and the West Riding of the County of Yorkshire, to be called the Blackburn Clitheroe & North Western Railway'. The Bill was brought in on 24 March and read for the first time on the following day; thereafter its passage was relatively easy and the scheme received the Royal Assent on 27 July 1846, despite opposition from the East Lancashire Railway (which had objected to the provision of a separate station in Blackburn).

The authorised route ran from Blackburn to Clitheroe, Elslack and Long Preston, where it was proposed that a junction would be made with the Little NWR. To the south, the Blackburn Darwen & Bolton Railway would form a convenient outlet towards Manchester, though the route from Bolton to Long Preston could not be continuous, because Parliamentary consent for an independent line through Blackburn had been refused. It was agreed that, when complete, the Clitheroe line would be worked by the Lancashire & Yorkshire Railway.

Construction commenced at Clitheroe in December 1846, the ceremonial first sod being cut by Lord Ribblesdale. In common with many other Victorian railways, the Blackburn Clitheroe & North Western was forced to effect major economies during the economic crisis of 1846-49, and although good progress was made, the works were built as cheaply as possible. The line was well advanced by the early months of 1849, and on 10 February *The Railway Times* printed the following Engineer's Report:

'The line between Bolton and Blackburn was in good condition, and . . . every economy had been adopted in the construction of the works. On the portion of the line between Blackburn and Clitheroe, the works had in all cases proceeded satisfactorily and about five miles of the permanent way was laid. Wood was used where practicable for bridges, and although the cuttings and embankments were formed for a double line of rails, it had been resolved to open from Blackburn to Clitheroe with a single line of rails only, which could be accomplished by the end of the present year if funds were forthcoming.'

This forecast was, in the event, somewhat over-optimistic, and the first trains from Bolton to Chatburn did not run until Friday 21 June 1850. This event was preceded by a lavish ceremonial opening which had taken place on Thursday 20 June, and *The Railway Times* described the great day as follows:

'The ancient borough of Clitheroe has at length obtained some share of the great privilege now possessed by nearly every town of importance in the kingdom through the medium of railway communication. That portion of the line of the Bolton Blackburn Clitheroe and West Yorkshire Railway, between Blackburn and Clitheroe, was opened to the public on Friday 21st inst. To celebrate the means of developing the traffic of this interesting and important district a private trip took place the day previously, at the invitation of the contractors, Messrs Nowell, Hattersley, and Shaw, who also invited a large party of the influential inhabitants of the district to a most sumptuous collation at Whalley, in honour of the auspicious event.

'A little after two o'clock on Thursday, a train of about a dozen first-class carriages belonging to the Lancashire & Yorkshire Company, the lessees of the line, left the Blackburn station with a considerable number of ladies and gentlemen to enjoy their first trip on this line, which passes through a most interesting district. Having stayed at Whalley a short time, the train proceeded to Clitheroe, and from thence to Chatburn, about two miles, where there are numerous lime-kilns and many excellent beds of lime, for which the neighbourhood of Clitheroe has long been famed . . . sufficient time was afforded at Chatburn to permit the passengers to have a ramble in the village. On their return the train stopped at Whalley at four o'clock. The bells of the venerable parish church of Whalley rang merry peals in honour of the day, while flags floated from its steeple, from Clitheroe church and castle, and from numerous other places on the line.

'At Whalley a spacious marquée was erected close to the station, in which, by the hospitality of the contractors, a most *recherché* entertainment was provided. Nearly 200 ladies and gentlemen sat down, W. Shaw, Esq., being in the chair . . . the usual toasts were drunk, and the festive board was quitted for the pleasures of the dance, Southworth's excellent family band occupying the orchestra, and this amusement was kept up with much spirit until about eleven o'clock, return trains at that hour taking the guests to Blackburn and Clitheroe, there being also a train to Blackburn at nine.'

It seems, from the above report, that the opening day was an unparalleled success, but major problems arose on the following Saturday when, without prior warning, the East Lancashire blockaded the line at Blackburn and refused to let Lancashire & Yorkshire trains pass until the L&Y agreed to pay a heavy toll for the use of Blackburn station. This belligerent action may have been, at least in part, an understandable response to the Lancashire & Yorkshire company's earlier behaviour at Clifton Junction, but at the same time the Bolton Blackburn Clitheroe & West Yorkshire directors had done much to exacerbate the situation by giving public notice of their intentions to open the Clitheroe line without first consulting their counterparts on the East Lancashire board.

Whatever the origins of this unedifying dispute, the matter could easily have degenerated into a major riot. When the first train arrived on Saturday morning it was impeded by an East Lancashire Railway engineering train, and by a force of 200 rough-looking navvies armed with pick handles and shovels. In the words of *The Blackburn Standard*:

'When the first train from Clitheroe arrived on Saturday morning, it was found that a complete blockade of the points had been effected at the junction with the East Lancashire Railway near Messrs. Turner's mill at Daisy-field; and that upwards of 200 navvies had been brought on the ground by the East Lancashire Company, with several engines and a heavy train of stone wagons, to enforce an obstruction to the public — of whose convenience, by the way, the East Lancashire Railway have always professed to be peculiarly careful.

'This disgraceful blockade continued during Saturday, only one train being permitted to pass on payment of a very extravagant toll. But even that toll was subsequently refused, and a notice was given to the Bolton company that their engine would be removed from the line in case they attempted to pass again over the East Lancashire Company's railway, because, forsooth, it had not been certified by the East Lancashire Company's Engineer . . . this legal quibble, nevertheless, proved more than even the East Lancashire Company could maintain; and on Monday morning, after a very significant hint from Captain Laws, the Managing Director of the Lancashire & Yorkshire Railway Company, that a game had been commenced at which two companies might very well play, the East Lancashire Company withdrew their "objection", and the Bolton Company's trains have since been allowed to pass on payment, under protest, of such toll as the East Lancashire Company thought proper to demand.'

The paper ended its report by criticising the East Lancashire Railway's directors for bringing together a dangerous body of 'ignorant navigators' and plying them with beer 'for no peaceable object'.

The East Lancashire and Lancashire & Yorkshire railways eventually settled down as uneasy neighbours at Blackburn (and elsewhere) but in the end all matters of dispute were resolved in 1859 when the East Lancashire directors agreed to merge their undertaking with the L&Y. At the same time, the former Blackburn Clitheroe & North Western Junction Railway was merged with the united

Right:
Double-headed 40s: 40122/D200 and 40091 leave Wilpshire Tunnel, near Blackburn, with the southbound 'Skirl o' the Pipes' railtour on 13 May 1984. *Tom Heavyside*

Above:
**West Coast diversion — Class 47 No 47533 crosses Whalley
Viaduct, between Blackburn and Hellifield, with the diverted
'Royal Scot' (10.40 Glasgow-Euston) on 2 April 1988.** *Les Nixon*

companies, these arrangements being legalised by an Act obtained on 13 August 1859 which formally dissolved the East Lancashire company and merged its capital with that of the Lancashire & Yorkshire Railway.

Later Developments

The complex web of lines in and around east Lancashire thereby came under Lancashire & Yorkshire control and in the next few years the enlarged company carried out many improvements, one of these innovations being an extension of the Clitheroe line, beyond its existing terminus at Chatburn, to a junction with the Midland Railway at Hellifield. The extension was built under powers obtained on 24 July 1871, but opening throughout to Hellifield was delayed pending completion of a Midland station there, and for several months all services terminated at Gisburn. Finally, on 1 June 1880, the new line was opened throughout, and the Clitheroe route then became a useful cross-country link between the Midland and Lancashire & Yorkshire systems.

Although the L&Y operated recognised main line services between Manchester and Leeds, Liverpool and Manchester, and between Manchester and Southport, the company was not a main line in the sense that the LNWR or Midland Railways were main lines; the L&Y system had no great trunk routes, but instead it contained a multiplicity of interconnected branch and secondary routes, over which the company offered a variety of services to the public. (In this respect the old-time L&Y system had much in common with the present-day Southern Region.) There were, on the other hand, several distinct routes, among them the lines running north from Manchester to Accrington, Blackburn and Bolton, together with an east-to-west route from Hellifield to Accrington and thence to Preston.

The complex L&Y system enjoyed lavish train services; there were, for example, up to two dozen trains each way on

the line between Burnley and Colne during the 1880s, while by 1906, the company was providing additional railmotor services as a means of combating tramway competition. In 1910 the Colne line was served by 11 railmotor trips each way, plus a full service of over 20 longer-distance workings between Preston, Accrington and Colne; many of these trains continued through to Blackpool, Skipton or elsewhere – giving local travellers a truly splendid choice of trains and destinations throughout the Northwest.

In late summer the annual Wakes holidays brought much extra traffic, and by the early 20th century (by which time holidays with pay had become widespread) whole towns would migrate en masse to Blackpool or other seaside resorts during the two-week summer break. These annual migrations produced numerous additional trains, and it was usual, during the height of the season, for excursion trains to converge on Blackpool from all over the north-western textile-producing area. For railway enthusiasts, these workings were of particular interest in that all kinds of locomotive were pressed into service to cope with peak traffic, and lineside observers could never be *quite* sure what would appear at the head of each packed holiday special!

Sadly, the L&Y system suffered severe rationalisation during the notorious Beeching era, and by the end of the 1960s the once-busy network had been reduced to its present size and configuration, with complex suburban systems around Liverpool and Manchester – but few passenger lines in other, more rural areas.

The Preston to Colne line has escaped closure, and this former Lancashire & Yorkshire route now exists in splendid isolation as one of the few passenger-carrying lines for miles around. The Manchester to Blackburn line has also survived, but the former Midland route between Colne and Skipton was closed in February 1970, since when Colne has become the end of the line from Preston and Blackburn.

These sweeping closures left the Preston to Colne line with a service operated mainly by multiple-units, but this service was commendably frequent, and there have in recent years been about 19 trains each way. In May 1971, for instance, there were 19 services between Preston and Colne, and 18 workings in the reverse direction. Additionally, the line was served by a handful of short-distance services between Accrington and Colne or between Accrington and Blackburn, while a residual service of summer through trains traversed the line en route from Blackpool to West Yorkshire (or vice versa); these last-mentioned workings used the Copy Pit line between Rose Grove and Todmorden.

The summer 1988 timetable provided a similar pattern of services, with 19 trains each way on normal weekdays, including 12 through workings to Blackpool. Sunday services consist of seven up and seven down trips between Preston and Colne. Most trains are (at the time of writing) worked by new-generation diesel units such as the '142' class Pacers or '150/2' Sprinters.

Engineering work on the WCML has frequently brought diverted InterCity trains on to the Preston-Blackburn-Hellifield line, typical motive power being Class 47s; similarly, the Copy Pit line forms a useful path for excursions or diverted services, and for this reason the Colne line continues to see large main line diesel (or even preserved steam) locomotives.

Right:
At Gisburn, a 156yd tunnel takes the Blackburn-Hellifield line beneath the stately approach to a country house. Preserved 'A4' 4-6-2 No 4498 *Sir Nigel Gresley* emerges from the castellated portals with a Carnforth-Manchester working on 3 May 1980.
Tom Heavyside

Below:
Passing the site of the closed Newsholme station, Class 47 No 47553 heads southward through the Pennine foothills with the diverted 14.10 Glasgow-Euston on 3 May 1987.
Tom Heavyside

Along the Line from Preston to Colne

East Lancashire trains originally ran to and from the east side of Preston station, but as a result of main line electrification work carried out in the early 1970s, present-day Colne services now depart from Platforms 1 and 2, on the western side of the main line. Leaving Preston, trains run down the WCML in a southerly direction, crossing the River Ribble on an impressive bridge and then diverging southwestwards on to former East Lancashire metals at Farington Curve (formerly West) Junction. With the now singled route to Ormskirk visible to the right, Colne trains glide round Farington Curve, which takes them across the adjacent main line and on to an easterly heading.

Having crossed the WCML, the double-track ELR route passes the site of one of BR's last steam locomotive depots

at Lostock Hall (24C). The locomotive shed lasted until the very end of main line steam operation in 1968, and Lostock Hall station was closed in November 1969, although (following the growth of nearby housing estates) an attractive new Lostock Hall station was opened on 14 May 1984.

Accelerating away from Lostock Hall, trains immediately reach Lostock Hall Junction, where a connecting link from the WCML trails in from the right; this short spur is particularly useful in that it obviates a Preston reversal when the Settle & Carlisle route is in use during weekend engineering work on the former LNWR route.

Heading east through a semi-industrialised landscape, Colne trains soon reach Bamber Bridge (four miles from Preston), a two-platform stopping place with solid, stone station buildings on the westbound platform and a level crossing to the east. Now an unstaffed halt, Bamber Bridge retains much of interest for the enthusiast, including an unusual flat-roofed signal cabin which is squeezed between

the railway and an adjacent row of shops; its glazed upper storey juts over the running line, providing an excellent view of the railway and the busy road crossing. Nearby, a grain terminal provides a useful source of freight traffic on a line geared primarily to passenger operation.

From Bamber Bridge, the railway continues eastwards, crossing a succession of level crossings and climbing steadily at 1 in 100. There was, until September 1960, a station at Hoghton, but this stopping place is now closed, and after crossing the River Darwen trains come to a stand in the two-platform station at Pleasington (nine miles); now unstaffed, Pleasington was always a passenger-only station and no goods facilities were ever provided.

Cherry Tree, the next stop, is only a mile further on; situated in a leafy cutting, this prettily-named place was once the junction for a branch to Chorley jointly owned by the LNWR and L&Y. Opened on 1 December 1869, the branch was 7 miles 60 chains long, and was, at one time, used by LNWR through services between Euston and

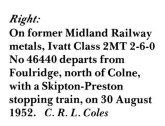

Blackburn; it was also used as a test run for newly-overhauled locomotives from Horwich works, but sadly, this picturesque line lost its passenger services in January 1960 and has since been closed to all traffic – the last section to close being that from Cherry Tree to the intermediate station of Feniscowles, which was abandoned in April 1968.

Entering the outskirts of Blackburn, trains pause briefly at Mill Hill (10¾ miles), the nearest station to the Blackburn Rovers football ground at Ewood Park. A short ascent at 1 in 100/1 in 130 then brings the line into the centre of Blackburn, and having passed a large coal depot and various other sidings and connections, trains come to rest beneath the double-span overall roof of Blackburn station.

Situated just 12 miles from Preston, Blackburn is the most important station en route to Colne, and it remains a busy local traffic centre, being served by trains to Colne, Preston, Manchester (via Bolton) and West Yorkshire (via the reopened Copy Pit line). All passenger traffic is now concentrated in the northernmost island platform, but a surprising amount of trackwork remains in place. For those with time to spare Blackburn, once regarded as *the* archetypal Lancashire mill town, itself comes as a surprise, for this industrial centre contains an Anglican cathedral, several public parks, an excellent art gallery and some delightful Georgian town houses in King Street.

Below:
On the climb out of Bolton, ex-S&DJR 2-8-0 No 13809 crosses Tonge Viaduct and heads for Blackburn with a Sheffield-Carnforth special on 31 October 1981. *Tom Heavyside*

The eastern exit from Blackburn is through a short tunnel, and beyond this, the DMUs reach Daisyfield Junction, where the freight and diversionary route to Clitheroe and Hellifield diverges sharply to the left. Daisyfield station (which had platforms on the Hellifield line but not on the Colne main line) was closed in November 1958.

Running through a traditional mill town landscape of terraced houses and steep hillsides, the route climbs at 1 in 118, as trains pass the side of Great Harwood Junction, where an alternative route to Burnley formerly diverged to the left. Nearing Rishton (15¼ miles) the line crosses the Leeds & Liverpool Canal for the first time; completed in 1816, this broad gauge waterway is itself a notable feat of civil engineering. Rishton station serves a small mill town that grew up in the 19th century around textile factories owned by the Petre family of nearby Dunkenhalgh.

Turning first south-eastwards, and then on to a more easterly heading, the route continues via Church & Oswaldtwistle (16½ miles). Interestingly, Church grew up around a calico printing works owned by the Peel family, and by the mid-19th century this part of the Lancashire textile region had developed into a specialised printing and chemical centre.

Accrington, the next station, is 17¾ miles from Preston, and once occupied a nodal position in the East Lancashire network, being the point at which the Blackburn Burnley Colne & Accrington Extension Railway converged with the line from Preston and Blackburn. In its heyday the station boasted a triangular layout, but today all trains use the sharply-curved Colne platforms. The station was partially modernised in 1970 when BR erected new buildings on the down side and removed most of the remaining Victorian infrastructure.

Leaving Accrington station, eastbound trains are carried high above the town on a huge curved viaduct with 21 stone arches, and having entered open country once more, the route reaches its summit near Huncoat station (18¾ miles). Although unstaffed, this station has retained its traditional gabled signal cabin in connection with an adjacent level crossing. With the M65 motorway running alongside, the line passes through Hapton, where the station has gained welcome additional traffic from a neighbouring housing estate. A short distance further on, the double-track railway unexpectedly quadruples (although the multiplicity of trackwork at this point is clearly far in excess of present-day requirements).

Rose Grove, the next stopping place is 21¾ miles from Preston; modernised in 1970, the present unstaffed station is merely a shadow of its former self. For steam enthusiasts, the air of melancholy is accentuated by the knowledge that Rose Grove motive power depot (which, like Lostock Hall, survived until August 1968) is now buried under the M65 motorway. At Gannow Junction, a mile further on, the newly-revived Copy Pit line parts company with the Colne route, and following the reopening of the former line on 13 October 1986 after a lengthy closure during landslip damage, the Colne line has been relegated to branch status.

Taking the left-hand line, Colne trains soon arrive at Burnley Barracks (22¾ miles), beyond which the route continues to Burnley Central over a long viaduct. Another severely down-graded station, Burnley Central was known for many years as Burnley Bank Top (the present name was railmotor stops in 1906, these simple halts were closed in September 1948 and December 1956 respectively. Running north-eastwards, the diesel units pause briefly at Brierfield (25½ miles from Preston) and Nelson (26¾ miles). Both stations are now severely rationalised, although Nelson has kept its original buildings and traditional canopies; the signal cabins at Brierfield and Chaffers Siding survive as crossing frames.

Beyond Nelson, the scenery becomes wilder and less industrialised, and with Pendle Hill looming mysteriously in the distance, trains cross a final viaduct before entering the spartan, single-platform terminus at Colne. Here, at a simple, unstaffed halt, the 30-mile journey from Preston comes to an end amidst spectacular moorland scenery on the borders of Lancashire and Yorkshire.

Top:
On the steep climb to Sough summit, '8F' 2-8-0 No 48036 is seen hard at work on a Manchester Brewery Sidings-Carlisle freight on 19 December 1967. Class 5 4-6-0 No 45381 is the banking locomotive. *Les Nixon*

Above:
New-generation motive power: a Class 142 Pacer DMU calls at Hall i' th' Wood station (between Bolton and Bromley Cross) with the 14.00 Manchester Victoria-Colne on 2 October 1986. *Tom Heavyside*

adopted in 1944). The once-thriving goods yard has disappeared, and a public park on the right-hand side of the line occupies the site of exchange sidings used in conjunction with a local colliery. This part of the line was double tracked between Gannow Junction and Nelson (Chaffers Siding) until December 1986, but singling operations carried out at the end of 1986 resulted in considerable track rationalisation, and the closure of Burnley Central signalbox.

From Burnley, the now-singled line begins its final ascent towards Colne, and with the Leeds & Liverpool Canal running parallel to the left, trains pass the sites of New Hall Bridge Halt and Reedley Hallows Halt; opened as

The Bolton-Clitheroe-Hellifield Line

In general, the Preston to Colne line has survived more or less intact, and although the northernmost extremity of the route has been reduced to 'basic railway' status, much of interest still remains on other parts of the line. Fate has been less kind to the neighbouring Manchester-Blackburn-Clitheroe route, but happily, the Manchester to Blackburn section has remained in being as a passenger route, while the northern continuation to Clitheroe and Hellifield may yet see a resurgence in its fortunes.

Present-day DMU services commence their journeys at Manchester Victoria, and travelling via Salford and Clifton, stopping trains reach Bolton in about 25min (slightly less if intermediate stops are omitted). At Bolton trains join the former Blackburn Darwen & Bolton Railway which, as we have seen, formed part of a trans-Pennine route through Blackburn and Clitheroe.

Formerly known as Bolton Trinity Street, Bolton station retained its huge, rambling Victorian buildings until 1987, but sadly, a much smaller, modern station has now been erected on the site, and apart from an Italianate clock tower, little of the original structure (apart from the platform buildings) now remains.

Departing from Bolton, Blackburn-bound DMUs negotiate a right-hand curve which takes them through a short tunnel and under Bolton's busy town centre. The first intermediate stopping place is now at Hall i' th' Wood; opened in 1986 this new station takes its unusual name from a late 15th century timber-framed house in which Samuel Crompton had lived from 1758 until 1782 (while working on his first spinning mule).

With the outskirts of Bolton now left behind, trains begin a long ascent towards open moorland, and soon reach Bromley Cross station. This two-platform stopping place is 2¾ miles from Bolton, and now marks the limit of double-track operation. Passing over a level crossing at the north end of the platforms, the DMUs continue northwards over a single line; the route climbs steadily at 1 in 73, and in steam days, the six miles of rising gradient between Bolton and Sough Tunnel were regarded as a daunting task for northbound freight workings.

Running through open country, the line passes the site of Turton & Edgworth station, which lost its passenger services in February 1961. Turton, to the east of the railway, was once a noted centre of the textile-bleaching industry; one of the local bleachworks was powered by an impressive, 60ft diameter water wheel. Nearby Turton Tower was the home of an old-time railway director who insisted that the approach road to his property should be carried across the railway by an ornamental bridge that still survives.

Still climbing, the route crosses a picturesque inlet of Wayoh Reservoir before trains reach the isolated and much-rationalised station at Entwistle (15¾ miles from Bolton). In its heyday this station had been situated on a quadruple-tracked section of line, but just one track now remains beside the windswept island platform.

Beyond Entwistle the gradient eases only slightly as the line, now running beside an old Roman road, reaches its 900ft summit. A deep cutting marks the southern approaches to Sough Tunnel which, with a length of 1 mile 255yd, is the longest in Lancashire. Coasting downhill, trains emerge from its north portal and immediately enter the built-up, outer environs of Darwen.

Serving another centre of the much-contracted textile industry, Darwen station is 9½ miles from Bolton, and retains some importance in that it is a passing place on the now-singled line between Bromley Cross and Blackburn. The spartan passenger facilities are typical of present-day BR secondary stations, but there is compensation in the fine views of Darwen and of distant Darwen Hill (Darwen Tower, sitting atop the 1,221ft hill, commemorates Queen Victoria's 1897 Diamond Jubilee). As trains leave Darwen passenger station they run through another passing loop serving a local paper mill; there has, however, been little traffic since 1985. Beyond, the railway passes an abandoned junction that once gave access to the Hoddlesden goods branch.

Still descending, the single line follows the winding River Darwen, passing the village of Lower Darwen, which lost its station in 1958. Within minutes, the DMU reaches Blackburn, and having crossed the Leeds & Liverpool Canal the route converges with the former Blackburn & Preston Railway at Bolton Junction. Blackburn station is only a short distance further on, and here, some 13¾ miles from Bolton, present-day journeys come to an end. The line from Blackburn to Hellifield is, on the other hand, still available for occasional use by excursions or other passenger workings, and it would be useful to conclude this examination of two Lancashire & Yorkshire routes by continuing northwards over the Clitheroe line.

Leaving the Colne line at Daisyfield Junction, the Clitheroe route turns through 90° and crosses the first of many bridges and viaducts. Beyond, the railway heads north-northwest for about a mile before a gentle curve takes the route on to a more easterly course. Rumbling beneath a series of overbridges, trains pass the site of Wilpshire (for Ribchester) station, and quickly reach Wilpshire Tunnel. Emerging into daylight the route then bears northeastwards to reach Langho and Whalley. At Whalley, the line crosses the Calder Valley on a remarkable, half-mile-long brick viaduct. This massive structure is one of the most imposing engineering features in the Northwest; consisting of a series of brick arches, it has one Gothic span (near the remains of Whalley Abbey) and numerous semi-circular spans which, on close examination, are seen to be of subtly-differing dimensions.

Having crossed this enduring monument to the Victorian age, trains follow the Ribble Valley for several miles. Clitheroe, once the most important intermediate stop, has retained its solid, stone station buildings, and substantial sections of the up and down platforms are still *in situ*. Originally closed on 10 September 1962, the station was re-opened on 8 April 1978, to cater specifically for those 'Dalesrail' excursions emanating from the Manchester area.

Below:
On the southern approach to Sough Tunnel, Stanier Class 5MT 4-6-0s Nos 45073 and 45156 *Ayrshire Yeomanry* **cross Entwistle Viaduct, on the Bolton-Blackburn line, with an enthusiasts' special on 28 July 1968.** *R. J. Farrell*

Above:
Stanier Class 5MT 4-6-0 No 45388 powers a Colne-Preston parcels working away from Accrington in July 1968.
D. H. Dyson

The range of destinations served has widened in the past decade, such as in July 1988 when the Ribble Valley Rail Group chartered a DMU for four Clitheroe-Preston return trips.

With Clitheroe Castle visible on its hilltop position to the east of the station, the railway curves towards the right as it approaches a private siding from Horrocksford Junction to the nearby Clitheroe cement works. As noted earlier in this chapter, Clitheroe was a centre of limestone quarrying even in pre-railway days, and this important local industry has continued to provide a useful source of bulk traffic for the Clitheroe line. Block trains of air-braked tank or hopper vehicles leave Clitheroe, on average, about four times a week, typical motive power on these company trains being Class 37 Co-Cos. The Ribblesdale Cement Co (now part of Rio Tinto Zinc) owns a small fleet of diesel shunting locomotives for use in its works, and this fleet included (until 1983) a Clayton Class 17 Co-Co that has since been transferred to the North Yorkshire Moors Railway.

Leaving Clitheroe, the line follows the Ribble Valley to Chatburn, from where the route continues northeastwards via the Swarside Beck Valley; Chatburn was the end of the line from Blackburn for over 30 years. In its heyday, Chatburn had been a classic country station, with substantial stone station buildings on one platform and smaller subsidiary waiting rooms on the other; both buildings sported projecting platform canopies, and an iron footbridge linked the up and down sides of the station. The goods yard was fully equipped with loading banks, a cattle dock and a five-ton yard crane.

From Chatburn the railway passes beneath Gisburn Park by means of a 156yd tunnel or covered way, and beyond this the line turns on to a more northerly course which takes it towards Hellifield. With the Ribble now running parallel to the left, the route curves leftwards in a great arc as it approaches its junction with the Leeds to Carlisle main line and, running on an embankment, trains pass over two road underbridges before finally joining the former Midland line at the southern end of the station complex.

As mentioned in Chapter Two, Hellifield consists of a long island platform, with terminal bays (now abandoned) at each end. Once a busy junction, the present station was opened on 1 June 1880, on which date the original Little NWR station became a goods depot. Until 1927 the station had been the site of two locomotive depots, but thereafter the old L&Y shed was closed and its allocation was transferred to the Midland sheds on the north side of the main line. It is interesting to note that former L&Y engines continued to be based at Hellifield throughout the 1930s, while a Horwich-designed 'Crab' 2-6-0 remained in residence until the postwar years. Other locomotives based here included the usual '3F' and '4F' 0-6-0s, together with Stanier Class 3MT 2-6-2Ts and Stanier or Fairburn Class 4MT 2-6-4Ts.

Hellifield shed was closed in 1963, and the station lost its goods facilities in the following year. Today, this downgraded junction must be one of the most depressing places on BR – although the station comes briefly to life when the Blackburn line is used for weekend diversions, and enthusiasts and photographers throng its otherwise-empty platform to see the rerouted West Coast expresses behind Class 47s or other large main line engines.

Having looked at some of the northern trans-Pennine routes it would now be appropriate to move south, in order to examine the Manchester to Leeds and Sheffield to Manchester lines. The following chapter will begin by looking at the L&Y main line between Manchester and Leeds.

Below:
En route to Skipton with an enthusiasts' special, Class 5MT 4-6-0s Nos 45447 and 45110 pass through Huncoat station on 17 March 1968. Today, the station buildings have disappeared, while the semaphore signals have given way to colour-lights.
Brian Stephenson

CHAPTER SIX

The Pennine Heartland: Leeds to Manchester

Traffic on the main lines connecting Lancashire and Yorkshire has always been heavy but, unlike the other lines covered in this book, their existence as through routes has never been threatened. Not surprisingly, the traffic on offer led to the construction of a variety of new lines and connections on both sides of the Pennines, but basically the two principal competitors in this central Pennine area were the Lancashire & Yorkshire and the London & North Western Railways.

Origins of the L&Y Route

Like the pioneering Newcastle & Carlisle line, the Manchester & Leeds Railway (M&L) was one of the earliest trans-Pennine routes. An abortive plan for a trans-Pennine route in the 1820s was followed, more than a decade later (and after a bitter struggle with the canal lobby) by the successful Manchester & Leeds scheme, which received the Royal Assent on 4 July 1836.

With a choice of routes available, George Stephenson, the company's chief engineer, attempted to keep the gradients as easy as possible, even at the expense of greater mileage; he adopted a circuitous route through Rochdale, and the Pennines were crossed at a height of less than 600ft, by using a glaciated valley at Littleborough. An interesting feature of the M&L contract was the involvement of other distinguished Victorian railway engineers such as Thomas Gooch (1808-1882) and John Brogden. The latter had special responsibility for viaducts and bridges, and no doubt his experience on the M&L helped when in 1851, he promoted the last link in the West Cumberland coastal chain – the Ulverston & Lancaster Railway – with its difficult estuary crossings. Another famous personality involved with the line was Daniel Gooch, who assisted his brother Thomas for a short period in 1836-37.

The first section of the M&L was opened from Manchester (Oldham Road) to Littleborough on 4 July 1839, with a daily service of seven trains each way. Opening throughout between Manchester and Normanton (where a junction with the North Midland Railway provided circuitous access to Leeds) took place on 1 March 1841. The completed railway was heavily engineered, and the aptly-named Summit Tunnel – 1 mile 1,125yd long and costing £300,000 – was the first tunnel of such a length anywhere in the world. East of the tunnel, the line followed the sinuous and steep-sided Calder Valley towards Elland, from where it continued to Normanton along the river's flood plain. The original route avoided both Halifax and Bradford, although by July 1844 an M&L branch to the former town had been completed; extension of this line to Bradford, again involving extensive tunnelling, took a further six years, but as a result, a further 70,000 people were added to the line's catchment area.

From a literary viewpoint, it is interesting to note that Branwell Brontë, the drunkard brother of novelists Emily, Charlotte and Anne, was employed as an 'assistant clerk in charge' (another term for assistant stationmaster) at

Below:
On a sunny evening in June 1987, Class 150 Sprinter DMU No 150251 arrives at Leeds with the 16.38 Scarborough-Bradford-Manchester. *Tom Heavyside*

Left:
A pair of Sprinter DMUs climb the steep bank out of Bradford with the 08.45 Blackpool North-Leeds on 20 June 1987. The former Bradford avoiding line (to Bowling Junction) can be seen on the left. *Tom Heavyside*

Below:
Lines between Manchester and Leeds, showing pre-Grouping ownership.

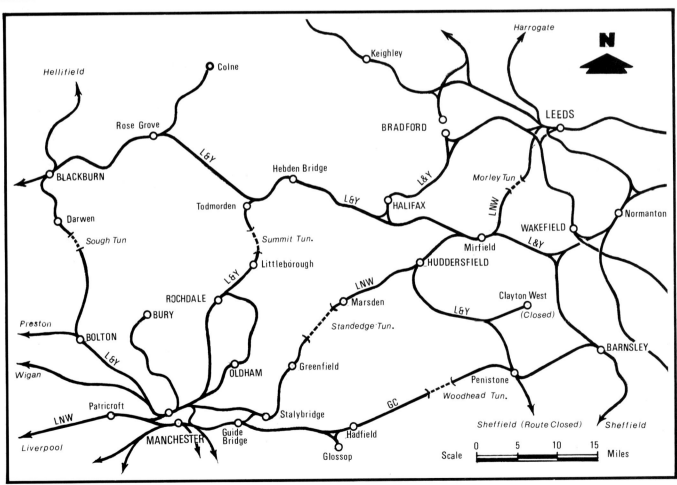

Sowerby Bridge station in August 1840. The following year, he was promoted to 'clerk in charge' of nearby Luddenden Foot station at an increased salary of £130 per annum, but sadly, Branwell seemed incapable of managing his staff, and when a subordinate was discovered to have stolen £11 1s 7d the unfortunate Branwell was dismissed.

On 9 July 1847, the Manchester & Leeds Railway changed its name to the Lancashire & Yorkshire Railway, and began to swallow up, one by one, various independent companies, such as the East Lancashire Railway (absorbed in 1859). Although little-loved by its customers during the early years (it was once described as 'probably the most degenerate railway in the kingdom') the L&Y continued to expand its operations, as instanced by the opening, in 1867, of the new Bradford Exchange station, jointly with the Great Northern Railway and twice as big as the previous building on the same site. During the period 1890 to 1911, the company further invested in its main line, with the provision of five running lines at Wakefield, and quadruple track thence to Brighouse, as well as numerous running loops west of that point. This resulted, to some extent, from increased traffic following the granting of running powers over the North Eastern Railway from Altofts Junction, thus enabling the L&Y to serve York, Scarborough and Newcastle.

Origins of the LNWR Line

There were, during the mid-19th century, persistent demands for a more direct route between Lancashire and Yorkshire than that offered by the M&L. Ironically the M&L, by declining to build a branch from Greetland to Huddersfield (then the most populous town in West Yorkshire, with a population of 25,000), prompted the formation of a local company to build a line from Heaton Lodge (Mirfield) to that town. The LNWR, anxious to secure its own trans-Pennine route, recognised the significance of this local company (by now named the Huddersfield & Manchester Railway) and had totally absorbed it by the time the Heaton Lodge-Huddersfield branch was opened on 3 August 1847. With a westward extension from Huddersfield across the Pennines towards Manchester now well advanced, the LNWR, through another subsidiary – the Leeds Dewsbury & Manchester Railway – turned its attention towards independent access to Leeds. This route was opened on 18 September 1848. Although heavily engineered, with a tunnel near Morley almost two miles long, and sharing L&Y metals for a short distance through Mirfield, it provided Mirfield-Leeds passengers with a much shorter journey of 12¼ miles as opposed to 22½ miles via the original route.

By linking up with the existing Manchester & Sheffield line at Stalybridge, to the east of Manchester, the LNWR's trans-Pennine route was completed on 1 August 1849. In contrast to the L&Y route, its gradients were much steeper, the ascent of the Tame Valley in the west resulting in gradients as steep as 1 in 125, while Manchester-bound trains were faced with more than seven miles of 1 in 100 between Huddersfield and the eastern portal of Standedge Tunnel. Set amid magnificent scenery the initial single-line tunnel was 3 miles 64yd long and was the longest in Britain from its opening in 1849 until the completion of the Severn

Top:
In the heart of the Pennines, Class 31 No 31200 passes the closed Hipperholme station with the Saturdays-only 11.17 Bridlington-Bradford on 19 July 1975. *Les Nixon*

Above:
The Pennine town of Halifax dominates this scene of Class 47 No 47083 *Orion* leaving the station with the 07.57 Weymouth-Bradford on 11 August 1979. *Les Nixon*

Tunnel in 1886. To meet expanding traffic, a second single-line tunnel was opened in 1870, to be followed later by a double-track bore in 1894. These widenings produced more than 15 miles of continuous quadruple track extending from Bradley, on the L&Y route, to Diggle, just west of Standedge, with the Micklehurst loop providing the same facility on to Stalybridge. As a result, freight and local

NER) beside the Midland's Wellington station; this new facility allowed through traffic between the LNWR and NER, and the present-day Leeds City station occupies the same site.

The LNWR's final flourish was even more spectacular, in that it involved construction of a brand-new main line between Mirfield and Leeds, the existing route being impossible to quadruple. The so-called Leeds New line used the Spen Valley (paralleling the L&Y Low Moor line for much of its length) and was heavily engineered, with 64 bridges and the 1 mile 571yd Gildersome Tunnel; the new railway was also steeply graded, with a climb out of Leeds as steep as 1 in 52. Opened to passengers on 1 October 1900, the line was primarily an express route, and although a local service operated, Gildersome station was closed early as 1921. Nonetheless, with four tracks now available in one form or another from Manchester to Leeds, the LNWR lines emerged from the Grouping as the frontrunner for central trans-Pennine traffic.

Above:
In a classic Pennine landscape, the unique Class 5MT 4-6-0 No 44767 (the only 'Black Five' fitted with Stephenson link motion) leaves Halifax with the 5.10pm Leeds Central-Liverpool Exchange on 17 August 1959, having just attached the Bradford portion. All the coaching stock seen in this view is of LMS design. *G. W. Morrison*

passenger traffic could now be segregated from express trains, thus permitting more traffic and smoother operation. Curiously, the tunnels contained water troughs, since they provided the only level track on the steeply-graded route.

Just as impressive as the tunnel was Huddersfield's new station, completed in 1848. Described by the late Sir John Betjeman as 'the most splendid station facade in England', the building was 400ft long and was dominated by a magnificent 68ft high portico with Corinthian columns. The LNWR was always keen to expand its traffic opportunities, and in 1869 it opened Leeds New station (jointly with the

Motive Power Details

Having used a variety of motive power since the mid-19th century, it was surprising that the L&Y should later have standardised on large, 7ft 3in diameter driving wheels for express passenger services (although the company's main line routes encompassed the relatively level Manchester-Blackpool as well as the trans-Pennine line). In 1891, Sir John Aspinall, the L&Y's Mechanical Engineer, introduced a new 4-4-0 class with wheels of this size, gradually replacing older 4-4-0s with 6ft diameter driving wheels; these locomotives were used extensively between Manchester and Leeds, and apparently could handle trains just as well as the 'six-footers'. From this promising start, Aspinall proceeded in 1899 to construct his unique 7ft 3in inside-cylinder Atlantics, 40 of which were built by 1902. Six years later, in 1908, one of Aspinall's successors, George

Below:
Heaton Lodge Junction in 1965 before remodelling, looking west: the Huddersfield line diverges leftwards. AWD 2-8-0 heads towards Wakefield light engine. *Les Nixon*

Right:
A Class 46 heads westwards through Brighouse on a wintry day in December 1983 with a Newcastle-Manchester Red Bank empty van train. In the background, the M62 motorway bridges the Calder Valley. *Les Nixon*

Below right:
The classical designs of the early railway builders are evident in this photograph of Class 45 No 45064 leaving Sowerby Bridge Tunnel with an eastbound freight on 20 April 1982. *Les Nixon*

Hughes, introduced the first of his four-cylinder 4-6-0s, and these in turn became front-rank motive power on trans-Pennine services.

Interestingly, some express services were handled by Aspinall 2-4-2Ts, and these tank engines turned in performances which were often indistinguishable from those of the larger 4-4-2s or 4-6-0s. This was undoubtedly because of their high tractive effort. A large number of these locomotives survived into the early days of British Railways, and fittingly one – 2-4-2T No 1008 – is now part of the National Collection.

With such potent motive power, the L&Y was able to offer highly competitive timings between the Lancashire and Yorkshire conurbations, albeit with often lightweight loads; in 1913, for example, the 9.40am Bradford-Manchester was allowed only 60min to cover the intervening 41.6 miles, inclusive of one stop at Halifax. Nearly 50 years later – in 1957 – the 9.15am Bradford-Liverpool took 75min to make the same journey,

although there were additional stops at Low Moor, Todmorden and Rochdale.

It is not widely known that, in the mid-19th century, both the L&Y and the LNWR were using *identical* motive power for their trans-Pennine expresses. John Ramsbottom's 2-4-0 express engines for the LNWR first appeared in 1866, and their performance on the steep gradients must have impressed the L&Y authorities, since the latter company purchased 10 of these locomotives from Crewe works in 1873. Between 1873 and 1896 F. W. Webb's 'Precedent' class 2-4-0s emerged from Crewe in considerable numbers, and could be seen on Leeds-Manchester workings until the advent of more powerful locomotives.

The first of George Whale's 4-6-0 'Experiment' class appeared in 1905, but the advent of a superheated version – the 'Prince of Wales' class – in 1911 meant that heavier trains could be handled. Between 1913 and 1921, C. J. Bowen-Cooke's 'Claughton' 4-6-0s began to appear on the LNWR trans-Pennine route in ever-increasing num-

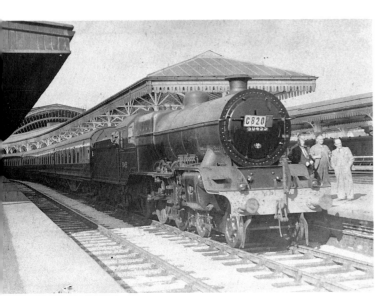

The last Hughes 4-6-0 in service is pictured at York on its farewell special to Blackpool over the old L&Y route to Manchester, on 1 July 1951. *R. Hogan*

bers, but small boilers limited their haulage capabilities, and double-heading with an 'Experiment' or 'Prince of Wales' was often required.

The 1923 Grouping inevitably meant rationalisation and standardisation, particularly as the L&Y and the LNWR were both now part of the LMS. 'Claughtons' and Hughes 4-6-0s gradually gave way to Fowler's 'Royal Scot' and Stanier's 'Jubilee' 4-6-0s, while, from 1934 onwards, the latter's '5MT' 'Black Five' 4-6-0s began to appear. On the freight side, lingering pre-Grouping influences took much longer to eradicate, with ex-LNWR 'G1', 'G2' and 'G2a' 0-8-0s and (to a lesser extent) ex-L&Y '6F' and '7F' 0-8-0s surviving until the BR era.

Initially, nationalisation in 1948 produced few changes. The final passing of the L&Y express era came on 1 July 1951, when the last Hughes 4-6-0 (by then numbered 50455) worked a farewell special over the old L&Y route between Manchester and York – an event to be repeated many times in the coming years, such as on 12 May 1956, when the Ian Allan 'Pennine Pullman' special, originating from Marylebone, was worked over the Calder Valley line behind ex-Great Central 'Director' 4-4-0s Nos 62662 *Prince of Wales* and 62664 *Princess Mary*. Similarly, on 26 April 1958, the same company operated its 'Pennine Limited' special between Leeds and Stockport via the Standedge route, this time using ex-Midland 'Compound' 4-4-0s Nos 41100 and 41063.

While the last years of steam on both routes saw expresses hauled by the usual 'Jubilee', 'Patriot', 'Royal Scot' and 'Black Five' 4-6-0s, double-heading was still prevalent, and on 10 April 1958, the 10.05 Newcastle-Liverpool (via Huddersfield) was worked from Leeds to Manchester behind 'Royal Scot' 4-6-0 No 46118 *Royal Welch Fusilier* and Patriot 4-6-0 No 45525 *Colwyn Bay*. Later in the year, on 22 October, the same train was double-headed by 'Britannia' Pacific No 70043 *Lord Kitchener* and 'Royal Scot' No 46146 *The Artists' Rifleman*, the Pacific having worked the previous night's Crewe-York mail train and then the 07.35 York-Leeds. Earlier in the decade, on 19 August 1953, a

more curious combination was noted on a Sowerby Bridge-Halifax-Morecambe Promenade excursion, double-headed by 'Jubilee' 4-6-0 No 45638 *Zanzibar* and 'N1' 0-6-2T No 69449; in this case, the 0-6-2T was attached as pilot between Halifax and Keighley, the train being routed over the steeply-graded Great Northern line via Queensbury. The 'N1s' seem to have been a rarity on this route, since the next recorded appearance of the class was on 21 April 1958, when No 69459 appeared at Sowerby Bridge on the 5.37am ex-Normanton.

One effect of nationalisation was the increased utilisation, mainly on the Calder Valley line, of ex-LNER motive power. On 11 June 1957, 'B1' 4-6-0 No 61387 powered the 8.30am Bradford Exchange-Blackpool as far as Accrington, returning almost immediately with the 10.55am Rose Grove-Laisterdyke empties, and the remainder of the summer saw a spate of similar workings, using locomotives based at Farnley Junction shed in Leeds. In the winter of 1959, Wakefield shed was allocated additional ex-LNER motive power; as a result, on 27 February 1959, '04' 2-8-0 No 63920 was seen on Sowerby Bridge shed, prior to heading a Greetland-Carlton ballast train, while, on 31 March 1959, Nos 63704 and 63763 of the same class double-headed a Barnsley to Mytholmroyd freight through the Calder Valley. More 'foreign' motive power was seen in the area following the transfer of 'K1' 2-6-0s to Low Moor shed in the spring of 1959. These

Below:
The factory chimneys of Sowerby Bridge dominate this June 1961 photograph of a York-Liverpool express, headed by an unidentified Stanier Class 5MT 4-6-0, about to enter Sowerby Bridge Tunnel. *G. W. Morrison*

locomotives seem to have been used extensively on summer excursions, such as Halifax-Manchester (Belle Vue) and Leeds-Llandudno trains, although, on 15 July 1959, No 62065 double-headed Class 2MT 2-6-2T No 41253 on the 2.57pm Bradford (Exchange)-Penistone train.

Both Manchester-Leeds routes saw their share of new Standard classes, introduced from 1951 onwards. Early arrivals, in late 1950, were brand-new '2MT' 2-6-2T Nos 84010-5, allocated to Low Moor for Leeds-Halifax local workings. 'Britannia' Pacifics were fairly regular performers on Newcastle-Liverpool workings west of Leeds, although their smaller sisters – the '6P5F' 'Clans' – were seldom seen, being generally used on Manchester/Liverpool-Glasgow trains; however, for five days in June 1958, No 72008 *Clan Macleod* was used on the 8.45am Bradford (Exchange)-Blackpool and the 7.30pm return, being serviced at Low Moor. From the mid-1950s '9F' 2-10-0s began to appear in the area, particularly on the Calder Valley coal trains, although the most numerous observations (as elsewhere) covered their use on summer-dated passenger workings such as Sheffield-Blackpool via the Calder Valley. Another class of locomotive used on summer excursion duties was the Stanier '8F' 2-8-0. For example, on Easter Monday 1954, seven members of the class headed West Yorkshire-Manchester (Belle Vue) excursions via Standedge, all carrying express headcodes, and entering the tunnel within 15min of each other. Ex-WD '8F' 2-8-0s also fulfilled a similar role, although not to the same extent as the Stanier locomotives or the '9Fs'. Well into the late 1950s ex-LNWR 0-8-0s could be seen working Calder Valley freights, with LMS '4F' and LNER 'J39' 0-6-0s representing more modern motive power on trans-Pennine workings between Leeds and Manchester.

Top:
Unusual Calder Valley motive power – 'A1' Pacific No 60114
W. P. Allen takes water at Sowerby Bridge with a West
Riding-Blackpool Illuminations special on 28 September 1963.
G. W. Morrison

Above:
A classic Calder Valley location: beneath the high skyline, the
11-car 13.30 Blackpool-Bradford-Castleford rounds the curves at
Luddenden Foot on 4 August 1979. Note the four-car Derby and
Metro-Cammell sets in the formation. *Les Nixon*

Right:
Emerging from the short Horsefall Tunnel, Class 45 No 45040
The King's Shropshire Light Infantry heads east for Healey Mills
with a fitted freight on 21 April 1982. The signals are controlled
from the distant Preston power box. *Les Nixon*

Right:
West of the Pennines, Class 2P 4-4-0 No 40588 pulls into Castleton station, on 3 June 1960, with the 3.47pm Rochdale-Wigan. The signals in the background indicate that the train is being routed via Bury and Bolton.
R. S. Greenwood

Left:
On the eastern approach to Summit Tunnel, the 12.26 York-Bradford-Manchester passes the village of Walsden on 14 June 1986.
Tom Heavyside

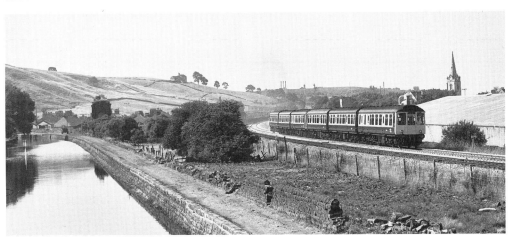

Left:
On the western approach to Summit Tunnel, a Manchester Victoria-Bradford working climbs out of Littleborough alongside the Rochdale Canal on 22 August 1983. *Les Nixon*

Below:
On 24 June 1987, a Class 150 Sprinter DMU calls at Castleton with the 08.55 Manchester-Scarborough. The pw depot can just be glimpsed through the bridge in the centre. *Tom Heavyside*

The Calder Valley Route Described

Present-day Sprinter units begin their trans-Pennine journeys in the extensively rebuilt station at Leeds, and the first few miles incorporate a section of the former Great Northern Railway. Running westwards, trains negotiate a series of complex junctions — a legacy of the many companies formerly serving the city — the last of which is the controversial Wortley West Junction, where the line from Wortley South Junction curves in from the left. This short stretch of line, allowing through running from Bradford to London without a Leeds reversal, was closed without notice in May 1985; a subsequent campaign forced BR to instigate a formal closure procedure and the long-awaited public enquiry was held on 22 March 1989. At the time of writing, no findings had been published, the double-track curve remains intact, although severed at the Wartley South Junction end.

On gradients as steep as 1 in 100, the line pushes through urban West Yorkshire, soon reaching New Pudsey station, 5¾ miles from Leeds. Opened on 6 March 1967, this station was initially seen as a replacement for the nearby Pudsey branch (closed in June 1964) but New Pudsey subsequently assumed greater importance as a main line 'Parkway' station. Hillfoot Tunnel is followed by a bridge which formerly carried the GNR Shipley branch over the line; this was closed to passengers in 1931, although a short section at the southern end survived for freight until the 1970s. The closed station of Laisterdyke marks the only level section on this stretch of line, and a spectacularly steep-sided cutting now marks the descent to Bradford,

Left:
Red Bank carriage and van sidings, just outside Manchester Victoria seen in December 1983. The Calder Valley line's approach to Manchester can be seen on the extreme right.
Les Nixon

Left:
Banking of eastbound trans-Pennine expresses up the 1 in 47/59 from Manchester Victoria was once commonplace – Class 2MT 2-6-0 No 46487 performs this duty in the early 1960s.
Kenneth Field

Below:
Through desolate countryside, Class 45 No 45017 makes the final approach to Copy Pit summit (749ft) with a Sunderland-Leeds-Keighley excursion on 22 March 1985.
Tom Heavyside

mainly at 1 in 50/58. At the eastern end of the cutting lies the site of Laisterdyke Junction and the former Bradford avoiding line, but in recent years, the junction has been removed, leaving the sole source of traffic — a scrapyard — to be served from Bowling Junction. Passing the closed DMU depot at Hammerton Street, trains begin a curving descent towards Mill Lane Junction and come to rest in the four-platform Bradford Interchange station, 9½ miles from Leeds; much smaller than its predecessor, it was opened in January 1973 as Bradford Exchange, but changed its name in March 1977 when an adjoining bus station was opened. Here the train reverses and immediately faces more than a mile at 1 in 50 as it climbs out of the basin in which Bradford sits, large tracts of wasteland bearing witness to the decline of the city as a railway centre. The city fades from view as the DMU passes Bowling Junction and disappears into Bowling Tunnel, nearly one mile long and one of several on the Halifax-Bradford section.

Emerging into pleasant countryside at the top of its ascent, the line quickly curves towards the site of Low Moor station, which was closed in June 1965, together with the ex-L&Y cross-country line to Mirfield and the Calder Valley; currently disused for much of its length, this route has been the subject of a recent (though uncertain) attempt to make it the focus of a West Yorkshire transport museum. At Low Moor, Bradford-Manchester expresses used to await the arrival of the Leeds portion, which had avoided Bradford via the Laisterdyke-Bowling line, but this is now a thing of the past as the train speeds downhill through Wyke Tunnel (1,365yd), quickly reaching the site of Wyke & Norwood Green station, from where yet another L&Y link to the Calder Valley line carried passengers until closure in September 1931.

Passing through Hipperholme and Beacon Hill Tunnels, the railway enters a dramatic landscape of which J. B. Priestley once wrote, 'Industrial man and nature sing a rum

Above:
The railway in the landscape – Pendle Hill (1,827ft) dominates Burnley (in the distance) as Class 37 No 37228 makes the steep climb to Copy Pit with a summer Saturday Blackpool North-Sheffield working on 24 July 1982. At the time, this trans-Pennine route was virtually disused. *Les Nixon*

sort of duet ... The factories might be roaring and steaming in the valleys ... but behind were those remote skylines ...'. Halifax, despite its reputation, has many fine buildings and is worth a visit, though the station, 17¾ miles from Leeds, has recently been reduced in size; few traces now remain of the spectacular Great Northern line from Keighley and Bradford, which once trailed in from the right.

With the urbanised hills closing in once more, the line is forced due south for nearly two miles as far as Dryclough Junction, where Manchester trains curve sharply to the right and enter the short Bank House Tunnel; the line ahead provides a connection to the eastbound Calder Valley line, currently freight-only (since the demise of the summer-dated 05.58 Bradford-Poole in 1986) although there is a campaign for its revival as part of a

Bradford-Halifax-Huddersfield-Barnsley-Sheffield through service. After crossing the River Calder, the line now joins the original Manchester & Leeds route at Milner Royd Junction.

'Beyond Halifax', wrote Priestley, 'are run desperate outposts like Sowerby Bridge and Luddenden Foot.' At Sowerby Bridge, 22 miles from Leeds, rail, road, the River Calder and the Rochdale Canal are hemmed in by gaunt grey mills, and by the Pennines, now rising to over 1,200ft, with houses clinging grimly to their sides; from here, a short branch once ran up the Ryburn Valley to Rishworth, but this was closed in July 1929. Near the station, on the right, lie the remains of a former motive power depot, that was once the haunt of massive Fowler 0-8-0s. Beyond this the line, still on gentle gradients, enters the 657yd Sowerby Bridge Tunnel.

Emerging into a greener landscape, dominated by Midgley Moor, the DMU halts at the small village of Mytholmroyd and quickly reaches Hebden Bridge (26½ miles). Extensive station buildings are provided here, and the staggered up and down platforms are linked by a subway. The goods yard has been removed, but happily the station was restored to its original condition, complete with L&Y nameboards, some years ago, complementing efforts made elsewhere in the town. Beyond Hebden Bridge, the valley narrows even more, the railway tunnelling directly through several rocky outcrops in a manner reminiscent of some secondary lines in the mountain areas of France. The last of these tunnels — the 225yd Millwood Tunnel — marks the approach to Todmorden; before the station, at Hall Royd Junction, the former L&Y route to Burnley and Preston curves away to the right. Known as the Copy Pit line, this scenic route climbs at 1 in 65/80 for 3½ miles into the wilds of the Forest of Rossendale before dropping to Burnley on gradients of 1 in 68/71 for 4⅜ miles; little-used for several years, it has seen a revival of Preston-Leeds services since 1984.

The station at Todmorden — 31 miles from Leeds, and a Lancashire-Yorkshire border town — was well provided with platform space by the L&Y, since it had to handle, in

Below:
Gradient Profile: Manchester-Halifax-Bradford-Leeds.
From **Gradient Profiles** *M29, M30 & M31*

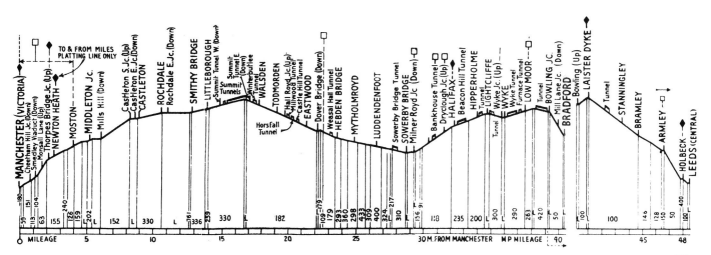

addition to main line traffic, local services from Burnley and Accrington which ran via a now-lifted west-to-south spur from Stansfield Hall. On a rising gradient of 1 in 182, the railway twists and turns southwards up a narrow valley ruggedly devoid of trees; on this section, the line crosses the Rochdale Canal twice. Beyond Walsden, the line dives into Winterbutlee Tunnel (306yd), emerges into a rocky cutting, then, after two more short tunnels, finally tops the climb from the Calder Valley and enters the 2,885yd Summit Tunnel. (The adjacent canal climbs over the hill by a series of locks.) The railway traverses much flatter terrain on the Lancashire side of the Calder Gap, but a glance back towards Yorkshire provides a good view of the distant Pennines. A 1 in 330 descent from the southern end of Summit Tunnel levels out just beyond Smithy Bridge station, closed in 1960, but reopened 24 years later by the Greater Manchester Passenger Transport Executive, through whose territory the line is now running.

Rochdale (39¾ miles) is another station much rationalised in recent years. A service from Manchester (via the Oldham loop) still survives, although the Shaw-Rochdale section was singled in 1980, and the Bacup branch — which reached 967ft (the highest point on the L&Y) — closed to passengers on 16 June 1947; the Bacup bay at Rochdale still survives, and is regularly used by terminating DMUs off the Oldham loop. Another now-forgotten service terminating at Rochdale was that from Bolton (Trinity Street) via Bury (Knowsley Street), which used the L&Y trans-Pennine route between Castleton and Rochdale; today, while the permanent way depot at Castleton still presents a busy scene, the line onwards to Bury lies rusting and derelict, with the Bury-Bolton section completely abandoned. (At the time of writing, proposals have been made to restore the Castleton-Bury section as a connection to the

Above:
With all the carriages in 'Trans-Pennine' livery, a Liverpool-Newcastle express runs through Morley behind a Class 47 on 5 March 1988. *Les Nixon*

preserved East Lancashire Railway, although costs have been estimated at 'several hundred thousand pounds'.)

Behind Castleton station (42 miles) the adjacent canal — also descending from its Pennine summit — almost reaches the railway embankment, en route to its own final junction with the Manchester Ship Canal. The railway itself falls

Below:
The Deltic era – Class 55 No 55009 *Alycidon* heads the 13.05 Liverpool-York through Batley on a murky December day in 1981. *Tom Heavyside*

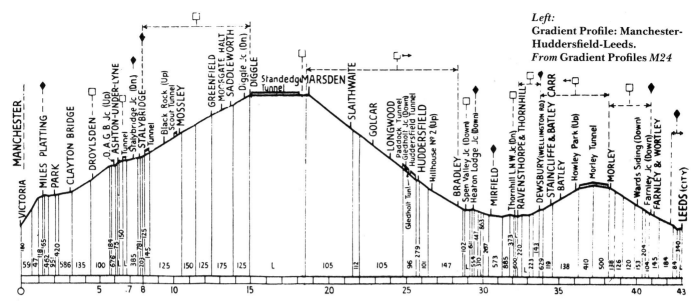

Left:
**Gradient Profile: Manchester-
Huddersfield-Leeds.**
From **Gradient Profiles** *M24*

steadily towards central Manchester, and the gradient sharpens to 1 in 152 down to Middleton Junction, where the station was closed on 1 January 1966, although the short branch to the British Fuel Company's coal depot remains in use; this line once continued to Oldham via the notorious 1 in 27 Werneth incline.

Still on a downgrade, the train enters Manchester's suburbs, passing the large DMU depot at Newton Heath

before reaching Thorpes Bridge Junction, the dividing point of the original route into Manchester Victoria via Miles Platting and the newer line via Cheetham Hill Junction. Taking the right-hand fork, trains drop steeply at 1 in 63, running through the short Queen's Road Tunnel before passing beneath the Bury line, still electrified on the third rail system at 1,200V dc. A little-used connection from the electrified line trails in from the right as the train passes the carriage sidings at Red Bank and crosses Victoria East Junction — the other end of the Miles Platting line — before coming to rest in Manchester Victoria station, 50¾ miles from Leeds. This impressive station replaced the Manchester & Leeds Railway's original Oldham Road terminus in 1844, at the same time making an end-on connection with the Liverpool & Manchester's extension from Ordsall Lane. With an overall length of 852ft, it was at that time the largest station in the country.

The Standedge Route

Trans-Pennine expresses taking the Huddersfield route use the same exit from the Yorkshire city as Bradford trains, as far as Holbeck East Junction. Here, the line diverges leftwards, first of all running parallel to the Great Northern's London route before passing beneath it near the site of Farnley & Wortley station (closed in November 1952, and situated on the old 'viaduct' route from Leeds New station). The gradient steepens to 1 in 104 as the train passes Farnley Junction, still serving the branch to Dunlop & Rankin's steel depot but once having greater significance as the starting point for the Leeds New line until its total

Above left:
Heading the 12.00 Scarborough-Manchester Victoria, Class 40 No 40195 runs through Ravensthorpe station and joins the Calder Valley main line at Thornhill L&NW Junction, on 30 July 1983. *Tom Heavyside*

Left:
On 26 June 1976, Class 40 No 40050 heads a summer Saturdays-only train west, towards Manchester, at Bradley Junction. Empty ballast shows that this was once a four-track layout. *Les Nixon*

Above:
English Electric Class 40 diesel electric sweeps down through the outskirts of Huddersfield with a summer Saturdays-only Manchester Victoria-Scarborough train. The location is of interest in that the former LNWR four-track line has been reduced to two, while the overbridge abutments are two of the few remaining reminders of the erstwhile Midland Railway branch into Huddersfield. Photographed in July 1976. *Les Nixon*

Above left:
Romanian-built Class 56 No 56006 passes Deighton, east of Huddersfield, on 30 July 1983 with an empty MGR train from Fiddlers Ferry near Widnes. Two years previously, this train would have been routed via the Woodhead line.
Tom Heavyside

Left:
A classic trans-Pennine express combination a 'Royal Scot' class 4-6-0 No 46127 *Old Contemptibles* and 'Jubilee' class 4-6-0 No 45563 *Australia* leaves Hudderfield with the 17.00 Liverpool-Newcastle on a sunny evening in June 1960.
J. R. Carter

closure in August 1965. Continuing on the upgrade out of the Aire Valley, the line briefly passes through open countryside before crossing the New line, at the same time being crossed itself by the M621 motorway. A long arc to avoid higher land in the vicinity of Churwell brings the trains into Morley station, five miles from Leeds and named Morley Low until closure of Morley Top (on the higher-level Great Northern route through the town) in January 1961.

Below:
A 'Trans-Pennine' DMU climbs past Golcar, west of Huddersfield, with a Hull-Liverpool Lime Street working in February 1976. *Les Nixon*

Below right:
Amid the grandeur of the snow-covered hills, Class 45 No 45142 descends from Standedge Tunnel through the isolated settlement at Marsden, with a Liverpool-Newcastle train on 22 February 1986. *Tom Heavyside*

Morley Tunnel (1mile 609yd) marks the summit of the climb from Leeds, the change of grade occurring almost halfway through — one of the tunnel's ventilation shafts is a distinctive feature beside the M62 motorway running across the top of the hill. Batley station (recently de-staffed amid much controversy) was once a junction with the complex of now-vanished Great Northern lines between Wakefield and Bradford, while the LNWR's short branch to Birstall closed as long ago as January 1917.

The Pennines appear as an unbroken line on the horizon as the train continues its descent at 1 in 119/138 through a typical townscape of millstone grit homes and large mills. Dewsbury, the next stop, was once served by no fewer than four railway companies — the GNR, L&Y, Midland and the LNWR, whose Wellington station (9¼ miles) is now the sole survivor. Of these diverse lines, perhaps the most interesting was the Midland, since the Dewsbury branch was part of a much grander 1898 scheme to build a Royston-Bradford main line, thereby avoiding Leeds and providing a truly fast route to Scotland; by 1905 rising costs

had forced the Midland to reconsider the entire scheme, and only the Royston-Thornhill section was built, together with the Dewsbury branch.

From Dewsbury, the line descends towards the Calder Valley, making its first crossing of the river before bridging the previously-mentioned L&Y line from Bowling Junction; this section until recently saw traffic for the oil terminal at Liversedge. A right-hand curve brings the express through the platforms at Ravensthorpe (formerly Ravensthorpe & Thornhill) and on to LNWR metals at Thornhill LNW Junction. For three miles, and passing Mirfield en route, an impressive four-track layout parallels the Calder until reaching one of the most important railway junctions in West Yorkshire — Heaton Lodge. Here, the original junction between the L&Y and the LNWR was flat, causing an enormous number of conflicting movements between heavy freight traffic using the Calder Valley line east of Wakefield and expanding LNWR traffic between Huddersfield and Leeds. This situation continued until 1970, when BR remodelled Heaton Lodge Junction, incorporating the redundant 'Leeds New Line' underpass with a new short stretch of line, thus allowing the LNWR-route trains to use the northernmost pair of tracks from Thornhill and effectively segregating Huddersfield-Leeds and Sowerby Bridge-Wakefield traffic.

This 1970 rationalisation saw the line on to Huddersfield reduced from four tracks to two. Swinging beneath the Calder Valley line the train begins its long 10-mile climb into the Pennines and passes the site of Bradley station (closed in March 1950), where a now singled west-to-south spur from the Calder Valley route curves in from the right.

Above:

In steam days, Marsden station had extensive buildings, and four platforms. Class 5MT 4-6-0 No 44732 descends towards Huddersfield with a freight on the slow lines, on 30 December 1965. *Les Nixon*

Almost immediately, two red brick abutments mark the site of a bridge carrying the former Midland Railway branch from Mirfield to Huddersfield (Newtown); completed in 1910, and intended as a passenger route with a fine terminus, this line was a freight-only route throughout its existence, and was closed as early as 1937. Now climbing at 1 in 147 alongside a canal, the express runs through open countryside for a short distance, and passes a new station at Deighton (opened in the early 1980s); the original station of that name was on the Kirkburton branch, and was closed to passengers in July 1930.

Huddersfield station, 17¼ miles from Leeds, is approached over a lengthy viaduct. Its magnificent facade has been mentioned earlier in the chapter, but the platform side comes as rather an anticlimax, although the through roads and overall roof all contribute to the main line atmosphere.

The Penistone Branch

From the platform end, a 1 in 96 gradient leads into Springwood Tunnel, at the western end of which lies the junction with the Penistone branch. This 13-mile line — perhaps one of the most neglected Pennine links — was an

Above:
A Stanier Class 5MT 4-6-0 emerges from Standedge Tunnel and coasts down towards Huddersfield with an express freight, on 4 June 1966: the two single-line bores are now disused. The basin for the Huddersfield and Ashton Canal can be seen in the foreground, though the canal tunnel entrance is out of sight. *Brian Stephenson*

Above left:
Preserved Class 5MT 4-6-0 No 5000 drifts down through Diggle, with the Pennine ridge in the background, on a Hull-Chester steam special in May 1983. *Tom Heavyside*

Left:
Class 40 No 40024 *Lucania* heads an eastbound ICI tank train near Greenfield on 9 July 1983. *Tom Heavyside*

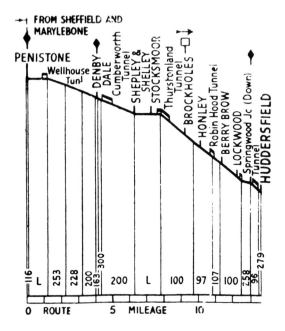

Above:
Gradient Profile: Penistone-Huddersfield.

isolated outpost of the L&Y, reached only by running powers over the LNWR from Bradley Wood Junction on the Calder Valley line. Opened on 1 July 1850, the line cuts across the grain of the country, resulting in steep gradients, impressive viaducts, and some lengthy tunnels, notably Thurstonland (1,631yd) between Brockholes and Stocksmoor; for such a rural line, the survival of all stations, apart from Berry Brow (closed in 1966), comes as a surprise, although two short branches to Meltham and Holmfirth, closed to passengers in May 1949 and November 1959 respectively. A 4-mile-long branch to Clayton West survived until the 1980s, mainly because of coal traffic from the collieries at Emley Moor and Park Mill; two abortive attempts were made to extend this line to the L&Y's Sheffield-Wakefield route at Darton. At Penistone, an impressive 31-arch viaduct straddling the infant River Don leads directly on to the sharply-curving L&Y platforms of the former junction station with the Great Central main line from Manchester to Sheffield — sadly a junction no longer after the total closure of the Hadfield to Penistone section in July 1981. In the Penistone line's heyday, through services from Bradford to Sheffield were entrusted to L&Y 4-6-0s, the star turn being the 10.00am Bradford to Marylebone. By 1918, there were no fewer than five trains between London and Bradford by this route, two of them with restaurant cars, though by the end of the 1950s the only daily survivor was the Marylebone-Bradford 'South Yorkshireman'.

On to Manchester

Returning to Springwood Junction, the LNWR route passes the short Gledholt Tunnel before settling down on 1 in 105 rising gradients for 6¼ miles to the summit, sharing the natural routeway of the Colne Valley with the adjoining Huddersfield and Ashton Canal and the A62 trunk road. With hills rising to over 1,000ft on both sides of the line, and with clear evidence of the removal of former slow lines, the

Top:
Just west of Greenfield, Class 40 No 40074 heads the 13.05 Liverpool-York on 18 July 1981. *Tom Heavyside*

Centre:
Snow-sprinkled hills make a good background to this shot of Class 45 No 45052 climbing past the small town of Greenfield with a Manchester-Leeds football excursion on 26 February 1977. *Les Nixon*

Above:
Houses climb the steep hillsides as Class 40 No 40084 drifts down through Mossley with a 10-coach train bound for Llandudno on 4 August 1979. *Les Nixon*

Left:
**Climbing from Stalybridge, a
Class 47/4 is about to enter
Scout Tunnel with a
Liverpool-York express on
24 July 1979. Note the
short-lived use of
air-conditioned stock on these
workings.** *Les Nixon*

line passes through a number of stations closed in October 1968, although modern housing developments led to the subsequent reopening of Slaithwaite. Several deep rock cuttings testify to the route's heavy engineering as trains approach the bleak settlement of Marsden, and, for the first time, passengers can see the Standedge Tunnel air shafts on the side of Pule Hill (1,385ft). Marsden station (24¼ miles) has lost most of its buildings, including the offices on the overbridge, but an LNWR signalbox controls access to a single line running loop extending for just over half a mile towards Standedge Tunnel mouth. Curving sharply to the southwest, the line enters the 3mile 64yd bore alongside the wharves of the Huddersfield & Ashton Canal, which now swings in towards the railway to cross the Pennines a few feet below the line's trackbed. The original single bore rail tunnnels, seen on the left, were closed to all traffic in October 1966.

Emerging into what was formerly Lancashire, trains leave the tunnel on a sharp curve and pass through the remains of Diggle station — another victim of the 1968 closures. A cutting shared with the canal, whose own tunnel is several hundred yards longer than that of the railway, brings the railway to Diggle Junction, where the Micklehurst loop (closed in September 1964) formerly diverged to the left. Diggle Junction once had a busy freight yard, but only the signalbox now remains.

Falling at 1 in 75, the line passes through a small upland gap to run across the picturesque Dobcross Viaduct, straddling both the canal and the small River Tame; at its southern end lies an abandoned branch to the upland village of Delph, from which passenger services were withdrawn in May 1955. The valley briefly widens, but Pennine scenery closes in again at Greenfield (30¼ miles), where the railway runs high above the rooftops of the small

Left:
**In early BR days, with the
Pennines clearly visible in the
background, Class 5MT 4-6-0
No 45201 approaches
Stalybridge on the
Micklehurst loop line, with a
summer holiday working.**
Kenneth Field

town. The contour lines force the railway into its sinuous course along the Tame Valley towards Mossley, a small Pennine town on the banks of the Tame.

Tunnelling through an intervening ridge of higher land, the line continues its curving descent at 1 in 125. On the opposite side of the valley lies a power station, which provided traffic for the southern end of the Micklehurst loop until 1972. Entering a tunnel beneath the northern outskirts of Stalybridge, the express soon emerges on the four-track approaches to the important junction station of Stalybridge, 35¼ miles from Leeds; this settlement was once an important cotton town, having been one of the first to employ steam power in its mills.

Pulling out of the station, Manchester expresses cross over on to the northern pair of tracks at Stalybridge No 2 Junction — a reminder that the route on to Manchester was built by the L&Y, the adjacent lines forming the LNWR route to Stockport via Guide Bridge, still well-used by a shuttle service. (In 1989 Leeds-Huddersfield-Manchester services were diverted on to the LNWR route, running via Guide Bridge and Ashburys to reach Manchester Piccadilly.) Ashton-under-Lyne, now much rationalised, is reached through a deep cutting and short tunnel.

Below:
In the early 1950s, Class 5MT 4-6-0 No 44927 climbs steadily through Honley, between Huddersfield and Penistone, with a Sunday Sowerby Bridge-Doncaster excursion. *Kennth Field*

Just west of Ashton station, an abandoned trackbed on the right marks the approach to Oldham Ashton & Guide Bridge Junction, named after the company jointly owned by the Great Central and LNWR. The section on to Guide Bridge, together with the west-to-south spur from Ashton Moss North Junction, remains open, though currently little-used. A 1 in 100 descent takes the train through the closed station at Droylsden, where the long-abandoned line from Denton Junction trails in from the left. A lengthy cutting leads into the valley of the River Medlock, once a scene of industrial despoilation, but now being transformed through the creation of a new country park. Appropriately, Park is the next station on the line, although most of its traffic is generated by an adjacent abattoir! Immediately after this station comes a triangular junction with a line from Ashburys, which once formed a direct link between Manchester's Victoria and London Road stations; having seen only spasmodic passenger traffic for many years, the line saw a brief renaissance in the 1980s when a number of Northwest-East Anglia trains travelled this way, but recent rerouteing via Stockport has resulted in a return to freight-only status.

A bridge over the Rochdale Canal and an array of semaphore signals heralds the approach of Miles Platting, another triangular junction, where the station buildings that were set in a 'V' formed by the converging Rochdale and Stalybridge lines have recently been demolished. The sharp curve means a substantial reduction in speed as trains reach the top of a 1 in 47/59 descent into Manchester; the trackbed of the line into the original Oldham Road terminus can be seen on the left. The huge towers of Strangeways prison can be seen on the right as the electrified line from Bury tunnels beneath the downgrade, and the crossing of the small River Irk marks the junction with the 'other' route from Leeds at Victoria East. Journey's end at Manchester Victoria, 42¾ miles from Leeds, is generally the lengthy Platform 11, giving easy access to the station concourse, with its wood-panelled booking office, well-restored refreshment room, and ceramic-tiled wall map of the Lancashire & Yorkshire Railway.

Above:
Class 40 No 40099 lifts its Llandudno-York train into Miles Platting on 3 July 1982: the lines on the left (now lifted) lead into the original Manchester & Leeds terminus at Oldham Road. *Les Nixon*

Right:
Almost on the roof of the Pennines, a two-car Class 101 DMU approaches Penistone (the station roof of which can be seen in the foreground) from Huddersfield, on 24 July 1974. *Philip D. Hawkins*

Below right:
A Class 101 DMU shunts into the L&Y platform at Penistone with a Huddersfield working in the summer of 1966. Both signalbox and semaphores have now gone, and beyond the platform ends, the line across the viaduct has been singled. *Les Nixon*

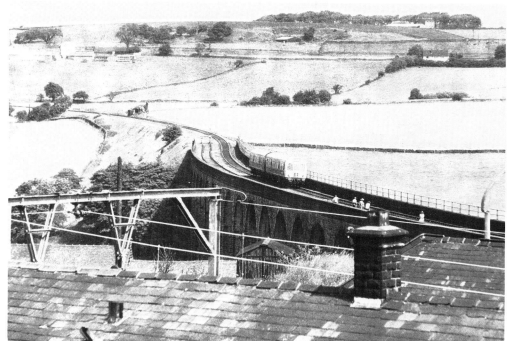

CHAPTER SEVEN

The Southern Crossing: Sheffield to Manchester

Unlike the Manchester-Leeds routes, which tapped several major population areas on both sides of the Pennines, no such benefits were likely to accrue to the promoters of any Manchester-Sheffield lines, and for this reason the Manchester Sheffield & Lincolnshire (MS&L) had this traffic to itself for nearly 50 years until the opening of the Midland's Hope Valley route at the end of the 19th century. Both routes became renowned for the beautiful scenery through which they passed, MS&L trains running up through the bleak hills of Longdendale, while the Hope Valley route passed through the more tranquil valleys of the northern Peak District.

Origins & Opening of the Woodhead Line

The very first proposals for a line linking Sheffield and Manchester had been put forward in 1813, when William Chapman suggested a combined canal and tramway scheme running via Dore and Totley, a forerunner of the Midland's much later scheme. If implemented, this early project would have provided a viable nucleus for future trans-Pennine developments, but in the event nothing tangible was done until the formation of a Sheffield & Manchester Railway Company in 1831. Sadly, the promoters of this scheme were unable to raise the necessary capital, but six years later, on 5 May 1837, a new Sheffield Ashton-under-Lyne & Manchester Railway obtained an Act for construction of the long hoped-for link; this new scheme envisaged a line running through Penistone, Woodhead and Dinting, with a major tunnel at Woodhead.

The first sod was cut by Lord Wharncliffe on 1 October 1838, and with Charles Blacker Vignoles (1793-1874) and Joseph Locke (1805-1860) as engineers, major construction was soon under way. Unfortunately, the two engineers were unable to work in harmony, and Vignoles eventually resigned in 1839, leaving Locke to carry on alone. In spite of this (and other) setbacks, the first section of line was opened between Manchester and Godley on 17 December 1841, and this initial section was extended to Dinting (then called Glossop) by 24 December 1842.

Meanwhile, work on Woodhead Tunnel proceeded apace, and a single line bore, 3 miles 22yd long, was ready for its Board of Trade inspection in December 1845; when passed by the Inspecting Officer, the Woodhead line was opened throughout from Sheffield (Bridgehouses) to Manchester (London Road) on 22 December 1845. (It is worth recalling here that the Sheffield Ashton-under-Lyne & Manchester promoters hoped to complete the whole line, *including* Woodhead Tunnel, for less than £1 million, although the finished cost was more than twice this amount.) The first train left Sheffield behind two new locomotives at 10.05am, and this inaugural special reached Dunford Bridge by 10.50am. With snow lying thick upon the ground, the train then proceeded towards the tunnel, and an accompanying *Illustrated London News* reporter noted that:

'It was 10¼ minutes in passing through this great subterranean bore; and on entering the "region of light" at Woodhead, the passengers gave three hearty cheers, making the mountains ring. It speedily passed over the wonderful viaduct at Dinting, and arrived at Manchester at a quarter past twelve, the band playing *See the Conquering Hero Comes*.'

The tunnel was opened to public traffic on the following day, and thereafter the Woodhead route became an integral part of the important trans-Pennine route between Sheffield and Manchester. For several years, the tunnel remained single, but on 2 February 1852, a second bore was brought into use; the original Sheffield, Ashton-under-Lyne and Manchester Railway had, by that time, been enlarged and renamed the Manchester Sheffield & Lincolnshire Railway. (In 1897 the more expansive title of Great Central Railway was adopted by the MS&L company.)

Manchester-Sheffield/Wath Electrification and the Woodhead Tunnel

While trans-Pennine passenger traffic was clearly valuable, the development of the Yorkshire coalfields in the late 19th century provided the financial bedrock for this section of the Great Central Railway. A large part of the coalfields' output was moved by rail over the Pennines to industrial Lancashire, loaded wagons being collected at the huge Wath marshalling yards (opened in 1907 to replace several smaller yards) and taken to Mottram yard on the eastern outskirts of Manchester. With over 40 coal trains a day on a steeply graded route (especially between Penistone, Barnsley and Wath), electrification was an attractive proposition. The GCR is known to have considered the

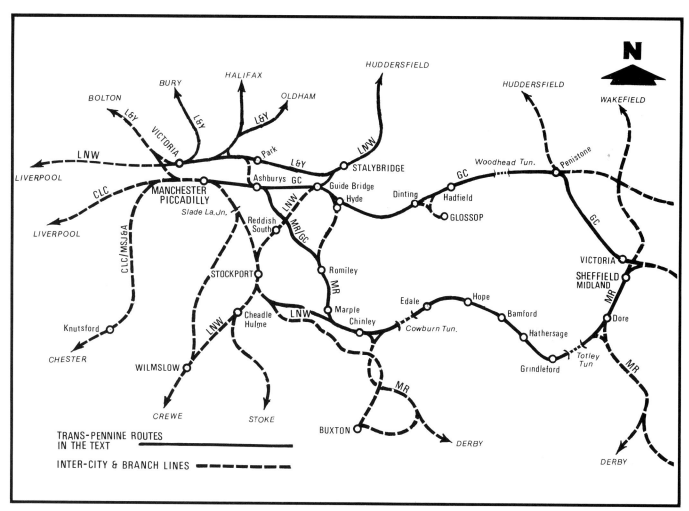

Above:

The Hope Valley and Woodhead routes.

idea, but no formal proposal was made until 1926 — by the LNER — and a further 10 years elapsed before the Manchester-Sheffield/Wath scheme was authorised.

Using the 1,500V dc overhead system, work on the project started in 1939 but was suspended during World War 2 (although the prototype Bo-Bo electric locomotive, later numbered E26000 and named *Tommy* was completed in 1941). Work was resumed in 1946, an early achievement being the boring of a short tunnel at Thurgoland (Penistone) to accommodate overhead line clearances. With construction of 57 additional 'EM1' class Bo-Bo electric locomotives now well advanced (the final 12 were given train-heating boilers in anticipation of a dual freight/passenger role), the first electric workings were inaugurated on 4 February 1952, over the 18-mile Wath to Dunford Bridge section; this portion involved the notorious Worsborough Bank, with its two miles at 1 in 40 against loaded westbound trains. Prior to electrification, four locomotives (two as train engines, two as bankers) were required over this section, but the new scheme halved motive power requirements and the Wath to Dunford Bridge journey time.

Right:

Woodhead in the 1970s – two air-braked Class 76s fitted for multiple operation are about to enter Woodhead Tunnel with eastbound MGR empies on 9 July 1977. *Tom Heavyside*

Left:
Great Central steam under the wires — on 24 October 1953, 'J11' Class 0-6-0 No 64435 leaves Mottram with a five-coach Hadfield-Manchester local. *Eric Oldham*

Centre left:
In a woodland setting, a Class 506 EMU crosses Broadbottom Viaduct on 22 October 1983 on a Glossop-Manchester Piccadilly working. *Les Nixon*

Bottom left:
In the early 1950s, before energisation of the 1,500V dc system, an ex-Great Central '04/8' 2-8-0 No 63781 heads a lengthy freight past Mottram Yard. *J. Davenport*

Top right:
The Manchester area always saw numerous inter-yard trip workings. Here 'Crab' 2-6-0 No 42760 heads away from Guide Bridge Liverpool Sidings under the wires with a Trafford Park freight. *G. Richard Parkes*

Centre right:
On 10 April 1982, 'Jubilee' 4-6-0 No 5690 *Leander* stands at Guide Bridge at the head of the 'Trans-Pennine Pullman' bound for Leeds. A Manchester-bound Class 506 EMU waits in the adjacent platform. *Tom Heavyside*

Right:
Woodhead express motive power — in the 1950s, black-liveried 'EM2' Class Co-Co electric No 27004 leaves Manchester London Road (later renamed Piccadilly) with a Sheffield-bound express. *The late Eric Treacy*

Far right:
On a damp night in the mid-1960s, Stanier Class 5MT No 44888 waits to leave Sheffield Midland with the 17.30 departure to Manchester, via the Hope Valley. *Les Nixon*

Left:
Class 45 No 45047 descends through the outskirts of Sheffield with a down working in July 1976.
Les Nixon

Bottom left:
Seen from a vantage point above the western portal, a Class 108 DMU pauses at Grindleford before entering Totley Tunnel on a New Mills-Sheffield working in August 1975. *Les Nixon*

Centre left:
Dwarfed by the ridge in the background, Stanier '8F' 2-8-0 No 48744 emerges from Totley Tunnel and takes its train into Grindleford sidings, on a wintry day in February 1966.
Les Nixon

Below left:
Nearly two years after withdrawal, ex-MSW Class 76s Nos 76030/51/34/27/25 are towed through Hope behind Class 47 No 47207 on 10 March 1983, en route to Rotherham for scrapping.
Les Nixon

Top right:
The beauty of the Hope Valley line — with the Pennines rising to over 2,000ft in the background, a Class 4P Compound 4-4-0 climbs from Bamford to Hathersage with an evening Chinley-Sheffield local on 30 May 1956.
R. E. Vincent

Centre right:
On 9 January 1982, a Class 123 'InterCity' DMU disturbs the fresh snow as it passes Earle's Sidings, near Hope, on a Sheffield-Manchester working. *Les Nixon*

Right:
Beneath the high peaks, Class 37 No 37209 heads east through Hope with the 15.15 Manchester Piccadilly-Harwich Parkeston Quay boat train on 21 July 1979.
Les Nixon

Left:
The great ridge penetrated by Cowburn Tunnel is seen to good effect in this photograph of Edale, taken on 21 March 1988. Here, Class 31/4 No 31438, on a Liverpool-Sheffield working, passes the next generation of Hope Valley motive power — a Class 156 DMU — just arrived with a press special.
Les Nixon

Left:
A lost route to London — a Class 45 heads along the Hope Valley line, near Edale, with the 18.06 Manchester Piccadilly-St Pancras train in June 1976. *Les Nixon*

Below left:
Shortly after leaving Cowburn Tunnel, immaculate Class 56 No 56125 approaches Chinley on 11 October 1984 with the High Speed Track Recording train, working from Chesterfield to Manchester.
Steve Turner

Bottom left:
With the Pennines dwarfing the western portal, a Class 123 'InterCity' DMU emerges from Cowburn Tunnel and runs downhill towards Chinley on 11 September 1982. *Tom Heavyside*

Top right:
Chinley North Junction on 15 September 1979, before track rationalisation — a Class 123 DMU heads a Manchester-Sheffield working on to the Hope Valley line while, in the background, Class 45 No 45001 waits to take the same route. *Les Nixon*

Right:
The Midland scene at Chinley, reflected in lower-quadrant semaphores, locomotive ('Jubilee' 4-6-0 No 45593 *Kolhapur*), and station buildings. Photographed in April 1967. *Les Nixon*

Left:
Class 40 No 40024 *Lucania* drifts through much-rationalised Chinley with a short van train on 24 September 1977. *Les Nixon*

Below left:
The 13.45 Manchester Piccadilly-Hull, led by a Class 105 DMU, crosses to the former Midland main line, from Manchester Central, at New Mills South Junction on 11 September 1982. *Tom Heavyside*

Top right:
The clean lines of Fowler's Class 4MT 2-6-4Ts are well illustrated in this photograph of No 42373 powering away from Chinley with a local train for Sheffield Midland, on 29 August 1959. *Alan H. Bryant*

Centre right:
On 14 April 1962, 'B1' class 4-6-0 No 61008 *Kudu* leaves Disley Tunnel with a lengthy train of mineral empties for Gowhole yard, near Chinley. *Alan H. Bryant*

Right:
The 15.22 Sheffield-Liverpool, headed by Class 31 No 31432, joins the ex-LNWR Buxton-Manchester line via the recently-constructed Hazel Grove Chord on 23 May 1987. The ex-Midland line, seen bridging the LNWR route, is mainly used by ICI trains to Northwich beyond this point. *Tom Heavyside*

The major engineering feat of this scheme was the boring of a new Woodhead Tunnel. The original plan had been to electrify the single bores, but the passage of 70 heavy freights daily in each direction was beginning to have its effect, and shocking atmospheric conditions in the tunnels were causing serious deterioration in the lining, as well as reducing the life of steel rails by 85% compared to those in the open air. By 1946, each tunnel had to be closed to traffic in turn for a period of nine months to allow the Civil Engineer to catch up on maintenance. Deterioration, however, was too far advanced, and one of the last decisions of the LNER was that it would be more economic to build a completely new tunnel, slightly longer than its predecessor, and at 3 miles 66yd, Britain's third longest tunnel.

In February 1949, work on the new tunnel commenced, taking 4½ years to complete. To house the 1,000 construction workers, a temporary township (shades of Ribblehead!) was set up at Dunford Bridge, complete with shop, post office, cinema and pub. Despite these amenities, the harsh conditions resulted in an annual labour turnover of 400%, and sadly six lives were lost during the construction phase. By October 1953, track had been laid through the tunnel, and its official opening to traffic took place on 14 June 1954, from which date all Manchester-Sheffield trains were electrically headed as far as Penistone. The tunnel was illuminated electrically throughout its length, and all steam locomotives were banned from passing through, although its later years saw limited movements by diesel traction.

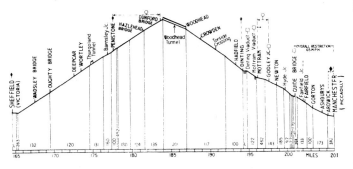

Above:
Gradient Profile: Sheffield-Penistone-Manchester.

With the seven express 'EM2' class electric Co-Co locomotives now available, the Penistone to Sheffield section was switched-on on 20 September 1954, allowing a full electric service between the two cities (the fastest trains were allowed only 56min for the difficult 41½ miles). Finally, the scheme was completed in January 1955, when electrification was extended for 4½ miles to the extensive Rotherwood Sidings; 65 route-miles and 318 track-miles had now been electrified in Britain's first trunk-line electrification scheme.

Optimists talked of an extension of the 1,500V dc scheme eastwards to the East Coast main line and southwards into the Midlands, but opinion was already swinging towards the now standard 25kV ac system and the only 1,500V dc extension (as late as 1965) was a short one, into the new Tinsley marshalling yard at Sheffield. Sadly, the combined effects of industrial changes and road competition led to an inevitable reduction in the volume of trans-Pennine passenger and goods traffic, and on Sunday 4 January 1970 the Woodhead route lost its through passenger services.

Electric-hauled coal traffic survived for several more years but finally, in July 1981, the Woodhead section was closed to all traffic, leaving residual local services between Manchester and Glossop, and from Huddersfield to Sheffield via Penistone.

Origins of the Hope Valley Route

The Midland Railway was a late comer to the southern trans-Pennine area, but in 1872 it began to stir itself and promoted a line from Dore, on the Sheffield-Chesterfield railway, to Hassop, near Bakewell. Nothing came of this proposal, and it took until 1888 before the MR obtained powers for a 21-mile line through the Hope Valley from Dore to Chinley. Apart from its scenic beauty, this new route was notable for its major tunnels, at Totley and Cowburn. Totley Tunnel, at 3 miles 950yd Britain's second longest railway tunnel, was bored so accurately that when the headings met in October 1892 the centreline was only 4½in out of line horizontally and 2¼in vertically. Cowburn was shorter than Totley Tunnel, being 2 miles 182yd in length; its construction nevertheless presented many problems and at one stage men had to work in flooded workings with the aid of diving bells.

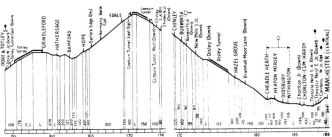

Above:
Gradient Profile: Sheffield-Chinley-Manchester.

Formally opened for passenger traffic on 1 June 1894, the Hope Valley line ran to Chinley, where it joined the spectacular Midland route from Derby to Manchester, which had opened three decades earlier on 1 February 1867 (when services from the south began running to Manchester London Road, via New Mills and the MS&L's Hyde branch). The New Mills to Hyde section came under MR/MS&L control in August 1872 when the Sheffield & Midland Committee was formed, subsequently becoming the Great Central & Midland Joint Committee on 22 July 1904. Further route mileage had been added on 2 August 1875, when the Joint line from Romiley to Ashburys (via Reddish) opened for passengers. On 1 July 1880 the Midland opened a new main line from New Mills South Junction to Manchester Central and the Joint line reverted to local status. In recent years, all services have used the New Mills-Ashburys route (following the closure of Manchester Central in 1969) although the opening of a new connection between the Midland and LNW routes at Hazel Grove in May 1986 has resulted in Manchester passenger traffic using most of the original route once more.

In the Hope Valley itself, mention should be made of a 3ft gauge railway, built in 1912 and running for several miles up the Derwent Valley in connection with the building of the reservoirs at Derwent and Ladybower. Over

1 million tons of stone were quarried near Grindleford, whence the MR carried them to Bamford, where there was an interchange with the reservoir railway. Construction work finished in 1916, and the line was dismantled shortly afterwards.

The Woodhead Route

Unlike its busy Midland neighbour on the other side of the city centre, Sheffield Victoria always had a much more relaxed air — a feature of many Great Central stations, including its London terminus at Marylebone. Despite the presence of overhead wires, the station retained its 'ridge-and-furrow' canopies until the very end, although one concession to the 1954 electrification was a modernisation of the booking hall and refreshment room.

After a mile of level track, during which an abandoned freight-only connection from the MR's goods yard emerged from the right, came a 19-mile climb to the eastern portal of Woodhead Tunnel on an average gradient of around 1 in 120. Neepsend station closed in October 1940, but the next station, at Wadsley Bridge (3½ miles from Victoria) though officially closed in June 1959, remains open for occasional football specials — Sheffield Wednesday football club's ground is nearby (a fact recorded on a BR blue station sign which survived into the early 1980s).

Sheffield was left behind as the line continued its climb through the River Don Valley, closely following the line of the river. Oughty Bridge station, further up the valley, was another victim of the 1959 closures; curiously, the small village it served, on the opposite bank of the Don, was always known as Oughtibridge. On steepening gradients, trains soon reached Deepcar, 8¾ miles from Sheffield and formerly named Deepcar for Stocksbridge; a 2½-mile-long branch runs west from here, along which occasional scrap trains still travel to the British Steel Corporation's steelworks. Happily, the gabled MS&L station buildings have remained in use as an attractive dwelling house, and the adjacent Great Central signal cabin has been immaculately repainted for use as a shunter's mess room; with its still-used ballast sidings behind the down platform, Deepcar retains a deceptive air of activity.

Beyond Deepcar, the track has now been lifted, though rusty catenaries and smashed colour-light signals provide a sad reminder of a once-important main line. The railway continued in a northerly direction through Wortley station (closed in May 1955) before turning northwestwards on slightly easier gradients. The long-abandoned Thurgoland goods branch curved away to the right just before the entrance to the short Thurgoland Tunnel. Beyond, the Don was crossed for the first and last time, as trains approached the junction with the line from Barnsley (now reopened for passenger and occasional freight traffic).

Penistone, 13¾ miles from Sheffield Victoria, was once an important junction with the L&Y line to Huddersfield, and the latter route remains open as part of the Huddersfield-Penistone-Barnsley-Sheffield service. The tall GCR Huddersfield Junction box survives to control the passing loop, and substantial station buildings, with the initials MSL in the ironwork supporting their canopies, stand in the 'V' of the two routes. A large canopy on the down main platform used to protect passengers from the worst of the Pennine weather.

From Penistone, trains ran due west, continuing to follow the Don Valley. Well-tended upland gave way to bleak moorland as the line approached the site of Hazlehead Bridge station; closed in March 1950 the station had been the junction with a steeply-graded mineral line to Crow Edge. Dunford Bridge, the next stop (19¾ miles), was over 1,000ft above sea level and this isolated station was extensively rebuilt on a new alignment during electrification, though with absurdly short platforms, which required trains generally to pull up twice. On virtually level track, trains entered a short cutting and headed through the 3 mile 66yd Woodhead Tunnel, beyond which the railway emerged into the upper reaches of Longdendale, immediately crossing the infant River Etherow. Alongside the track, the pylons carrying power supplies up Longdendale suddenly came to an end, the cables being routed thence across the Pennines through one of the abandoned 19th century bores — this function continues today. Woodhead station (22¾ miles) closed in July 1964; like Crowden, two miles down the valley, which closed in February 1957, it is difficult to see what traffic these very isolated stations could have attracted.

The bare, desolate hills of Longdendale rose up to more than 1,500ft as trains gathered speed down the 1 in 117 falling gradients. Once quadruple-tracked for some distance, the line skirted Woodhead, Torside, Rhodeswood, Valehouse and Bottoms reservoirs for a distance of nearly seven miles, partly on a ledge cut into the southern flank of the valley. Beyond Bottoms reservoir, Longdendale began to widen, and the village of Padfield, on the left, provided the first sign of any settlement since Penistone. Seconds later, trains ran into Hadfield, 29¼ miles from Sheffield Victoria and the present limit of electrified local services from Manchester. (This last section of the erstwhile Woodhead route now operates on the 25,000V ac system.) Hadfield's well-proportioned station building, built of Derbyshire stone, is in keeping with its surroundings, though its mock-Jacobean chimneys add a whimsical touch. Descending at 1 in 100, and still more than 500ft above sea level, trains head southward for a mile before taking the single line north-to-east curve at Dinting; in 'main line' days, all expresses took the direct route to Manchester, but through working via Dinting's main line platform is now much reduced.

As the railway begins to curve eastwards past the Dinting Railway Centre (home of 'Jubilee' class *Bahamas* and other steam locomotives) the great Pennine barrier looms once more on the horizon, with the little town of Glossop nestling at its foot; this was once a staging point at the foot of the notorious Snake Pass, one of the roads between Manchester and Sheffield. The terminus at Glossop lies a mile from the main line; only a single line survives, though the width of the overhead gantries suggests a once more extensive layout. From Glossop, trains retrace their path to the main line, and call at Dinting (30 miles from Sheffield via the direct route) before heading out on to the 1,452ft-long Dinting Viaduct; this impressive structure towers 125ft above the valley floor.

Pennine bleakness is replaced by rolling scenery as the line passes the sad remains of Mottram yard, seen on the left at a level several feet lower than the main line; a small platform, just west of the A626 road bridge, remained in use until recently for workers at the yard. Beyond the west end of the yard, and on easier gradients, trains cross

Broadbottom Viaduct before entering the station of the same name. Further on, a recently-opened station at Godley East has taken away much of the passenger traffic from Godley Junction (33¾ miles), which was formerly an important interchange point between the Woodhead route and the jointly-owned Cheshire Lines system.

The easternmost suburbs of Manchester are reached as the train descends at 1 in 143 across the M67, pausing briefly at the recently-renamed Newton for Hyde before running into the new and delightfully named Flowery Field station, adjacent to Hyde Junction, where the line from Romiley trails in from the left. A short run brings EMUs across the Tame Valley, along the base of a triangular junction with the Stalybridge line and into Guide Bridge station, 37 miles from Sheffield. Commodious buildings and four through platforms bear witness to its important role as an interchange station, not only with the Stockport to Stalybridge route, but also with an abandoned local service to Ashton-under-Lyne and Oldham.

Passing under the Denton-Ashton Moss line, EMUs soon reach Fairfield, from where it was once possible for the Woodhead Electrics to reach Reddish depot. Today, it is only possible to reach this line (which continues to Trafford Park) via the next station, Gorton (39 miles); here were situated the long-closed locomotive works of the Great Central. Still descending, at 1 in 173, through less prosperous Manchester suburbs, the line passes Ashburys for Belle Vue, the point of convergence with the line from New Mills and of divergence of the 'back line' to Manchester Victoria (mentioned in Chapter Six). With the skyline of Manchester's city centre (dominated by the towering Piccadilly Hotel) visible ahead, the London main line is quickly reached for the short run to the imposing Manchester Piccadilly station, 41¾ miles from Sheffield Victoria.

The Hope Valley Route Described

Leaving busy Sheffield Midland station, trains depart southwestwards for the five-mile climb up the River Sheaf valley. Steep hillsides, scarred at first by urban and industrial decay, are quickly enveloped in dense woodland as the line passes, on the right, a large millpond, downstream from which is the Abbeydale Industrial hamlet, the only surviving reminder of Sheffield's original cutlery industry. Approaching the unmanned Dore and Totley station, Manchester trains diverge westwards on to their own line on a gradient of 1 in 100 and, with the hills closing in on both sides, soon enter the gloomy eastern portal of Totley Tunnel. After several minutes of travelling beneath moors over 1,000ft high, a right-hand bend reveals the tunnel's western portal at Grindleford (9¾ miles). At all Hope Valley stations, wooden Midland Railway signalboxes survive, although the line's station buildings have been reduced to 'bus shelters', following a lengthy spate of vandalism around 1970.

The hills of the Peak District now determine the line's course as it runs high above the River Derwent before passing through woods and entering Hathersage station; Hathersage village, nestling in the steep hillside, is reputedly the birthplace of Little John of Robin Hood fame. Passing Bamford, trains cross the Derwent, heading down

from the massive Ladybower and Derwent reservoirs built during World War 1. From Hope station (14¾ miles), the line is funnelled between Lose Hill and Win Hill (both over 1,500ft) as it begins its 1 in 100 ascent of the Vale of Edale. The Hope Valley itself veers away to the west, the small village of Castleton at its head being famous for its Blue John caverns and lending itself to the station's full name – Hope for Castleton and Bradwell. A mile beyond Hope, a two-mile-long line branches leftwards to serve a large cement works.

Climbing into Edale, the line turns west once more through an awe-inspiring landscape, dominated by the mass of Kinder Scout, at 2,088ft the highest mountain in the Peak District. For many walkers, Edale station provides convenient access to the southern starting point of the Pennine Way, 250 miles of footpath to the Cheviot Hills of Southern Scotland. Running westwards, the line plunges into Cowburn Tunnel, its portal dwarfed by the 2,000ft Colborne Ridge which the tunnel must penetrate. Emerging at a gradient of 1 in 150/100 to pass the reinstated single-track spur to the freight-only Peak Forest line, Hope Valley trains join the latter route at Chinley (25¾ miles); now only a shadow of its former self, Chinley once boasted four through platforms together with two terminal bays. Along what was once a four-track layout, the line approaches New Mills South Junction, where the 1880 'new line' diverges to the left; the Manchester to Buxton route is visible on the far side of Furness Vale, high above the River Goyt and the Peak Forest Canal.

Until 1986, all trains climbed at 1 in 98 into a short tunnel, emerging to join a short stub of the former Hayfield branch before running into the rather constricted New Mills station. Heading northwest through attractive countryside with millstone grit cottages dotting the steep hillsides, the line crossed the Goyt, and ran through another short tunnel into Marple station, where the Rose Hill Marple branch converged from the left. Beyond, both railway and Peak Forest Canal (the latter on an aqueduct) crossed the Goyt Valley. At Romiley Junction, trains from Sheffield ran straight ahead, dropped through Bredbury station (35½ miles) and crossed the Stockport to Woodley line before passing the modern station at Brinnington, opened on 12 December 1977. Running under the LNWR Stockport-Stalybridge line, the train entered Manchester's suburbs. A further overbridge just beyond carried 1,500V dc electrified lines into Reddish depot (once the main shed for Woodhead services but now closed) and after Belle Vue station, the Woodhead line was joined at Ashburys.

The construction of a single-track curve in 1986 linked the freight-only 'new line' from New Mills South Junction and the Buxton-Stockport line, providing a better route into Manchester, both in terms of the approach to the terminus and of access to the through platforms at Piccadilly (most long-distance trains now continue to Liverpool). As a result, these workings now continue straight ahead at New Mills South, crossing the River Goyt as they drop at 1 in 100 into the attractive Furness Vale. Running alongside the Peak Forest Canal for a short distance, and with the Buxton line visible on the opposite bank, the line soon plunges into Disley Tunnel, at 2miles 346yd, the sixth longest in Britain; its name is carved in large letters above each portal. Emerging into a series of cuttings, the line is crossed by the abandoned Marple Rose Hill-Macclesfield line directly above the tunnel's western portal, though this is not easily

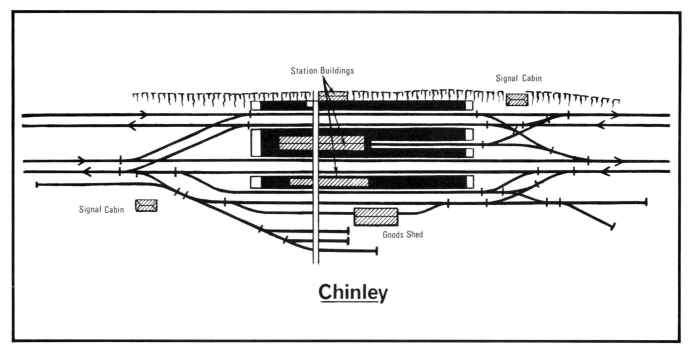

Chinley

Above:
Trackplan: Chinley before modernisation.

discernible. Just over a mile from the tunnel, trains slow for the new chord line, descending on a curve for half a mile to join the Buxton line just outside Hazel Grove station; in recent years, this line has been electrified from Edgeley Junction (Stockport) and some EMU services from Manchester Piccadilly now terminate here. Running through the southern suburbs of the Greater Manchester conurbation, a sharp right-hand curve brings trains through Edgeley Junction and on to the London main line for the short run to Stockport station, 36¾ miles from Sheffield.

Stockport retains an extensive track layout with its platforms, through roads, and bay platforms still in existence; wide canopies and commodious station buildings complete a scene of bustle and activity. The well known viaduct carries the line high across the River Tame, and at Heaton Norris Junction, where the Stalybridge line swings away rightwards, an old LNWR goods warehouse remains intact, though no longer rail-connected. Beyond Levenshulme station, the electrified Styal loop from Wilmslow converges from the left, beyond which trains pass the large motive power depot and carriage sidings at Longsight. Journey's end is near as Ardwick Junction is passed and the graceful curved outlines of the overall roof at Manchester Piccadilly (42¾ miles from Sheffield) come into view.

Below:
Class 45 No 45115 heads the 16.45 Liverpool Lime Street-Sheffield through Hazel Grove on 23 May 1987. The large car park caters for Manchester's growing commuter traffic.
Tom Heavyside

CHAPTER EIGHT

Towards the Future

In this final chapter, the opportunity is taken to review trans-Pennine rail developments since the early 1960s. Although closures of some of the lesser-used branches had already taken place — the isolated Hexham to Allendale Town branch, for example, had lost its passenger service as long ago as September 1930 — all the main trans-Pennine arteries remained intact until 1962. From then on, however, came 20 years of appraisal and change.

The Northern Lines – Tyneside/ Teesside to Cumbria

Following nationalisation, long-term prospects for both passenger and freight services between Darlington, Penrith and Tebay always looked bleak. The relatively small amount of freight was expensive to work, with double-heading needed for both east and west approaches to Stainmore, while the meagre passenger traffic on offer required only three trains daily each way between Darlington and Penrith (the Kirkby Stephen-Tebay line had already lost its passenger service in December 1952) — indeed, dieselisation of passenger services on this route in 1957 came as a surprise to some observers.

BR first proposed closure in 1960, maintaining that coke traffic from County Durham to the iron and steel works at Barrow-in-Furness and Millom could be routed via the Newcastle and Carlisle line, Workington and Whitehaven. Introduced on an experimental basis in July 1960, this change was an immediate success and heralded the end of the Stainmore route. (In any case, a changed sourcing pattern meant that the Furness iron and steel industry was beginning to use more West Riding coke, which was moved via Leeds, Skipton, Wennington and the Furness & Midland Joint line.) The major goods traffic originating on the route — limestone from Merrygill quarry and Ministry of Defence traffic from Warcop — could be handled on the section between Appleby and Kirkby Stephen, which it was proposed to keep open for freight, although, as most of the limestone was used in the Teesside blast furnaces, the new route via Carlisle involved about three times the mileage over Stainmore.

The closure proposals were not bitterly contested, and the fact that no new bus services were required vindicated BR's claim that traffic was light. The last trains ran between Penrith and Barnard Castle in January 1962, most of the track being lifted very quickly, although the passenger service between Darlington and Barnard Castle

held out a little longer, not succumbing until 30 November 1964.

West of Penrith, the CK&P section was not part of the Stainmore closure proposals, although, despite dieselisation in the 1950s, the route was considered to be a loss maker. The 1963 Beeching Report recommended total closure between Penrith and Workington, a situation not helped by the withdrawal of most freight services in 1964. Initially, however, only the Keswick-Workington portion, with its scenic section alongside Bassenthwaite Lake, was closed — on Saturday 16 April 1966 — the Minister of Transport refusing to sanction closure of the route between Keswick and the WCML. Despite further rationalisation, however, which reduced Keswick-Penrith to a single-line 'long siding', the closure case was eventually resubmitted, the last passenger trains running on Saturday 4 March 1972. In retrospect, BR seem to have pushed through closure with almost indecent haste — two years later the WCML from Euston was electrified throughout, and would have given an attractive time of around $4\frac{1}{2}$hr between London and Keswick.

Closure of the Stainmore route, with the diversion of its freight traffic, made the future of the Newcastle-Carlisle line even more secure. Another early dieselisation candidate — by the late 1950s, four-car Metro-Cammell DMUs, complete with buffet car, were working between the two cities — the level of through services has remained remarkably constant over the last 20 years, as the table below shows:

	1971	1979	1988
Number of Trains Newcastle-Carlisle	12	11	11
Number of Trains Newcastle-Hexham/Haltwhistle	14	21	19
Fastest Journey Time (min)	89	89	90

The 1971 service included summer Saturday locomotive-hauled workings to Stranraer Harbour and to Blackpool, the latter being the direct descendant of the Blackpool working via Stainmore: both had been withdrawn by the mid-1970s. The 50% increase in Newcastle-Hexham services between 1971 and 1979 reflects the influence of the Tyne & Wear Passenger Transport Executive, to which financial support for these local services had now passed.

Post-1960 developments on this route have not been as exciting as those on other trans-Pennine lines as the above table shows, but this might not always have been the case

— the 1965 revised plan for the *Re-shaping of British Railways* (the so-called Beeching II) raised the intriguing possibility of closure of the East Coast main line north of Newcastle, Anglo-Scottish trains from King's Cross then being permanently re-routed via the N&CR route. (This option was later rejected.) The original 1963 Beeching Plan, however, proposed closure of most intermediate stations between Newcastle and Carlisle, together with total closure of the Haltwhistle-Alston branch. The latter proposal was soon withdrawn, because of the poor roads in the South Tyne Valley, but closure was again put forward in August 1970, when plans to improve the A689 as an 'all-weather' road to the high market town were announced. However, building the road took longer than anticipated, closure of the branch not finally taking place until 1 May 1976. Today, rails are back in the valley, the South Tynedale Railway Preservation Society gradually pushing its 2ft gauge line northwards from Alston along the old trackbed.

The outcome of the closure proposals on the main line, however, was rather different. On 3 January 1966, the North Eastern Region announced the closure of 10 intermediate stations between Newcastle and Carlisle, but three of these — Blaydon, Wylam and Bardon Mill — were reprieved nine months later, while a fourth — Wetheral — was reopened in October 1981 to serve an expanding village on the outskirts of Carlisle.

The eastern end of the route has also been characterised by line closures and reopenings. Between Scotswood Junction and West Wylam Junction, double-track lines ran along both banks of the Tyne, but the northerly route was closed from 11 March 1968, most of the intermediate stations having lost their services 10 years earlier. A further change was made in the early 1980s, when services east of Blaydon were re-routed into Newcastle via the former freight-only lines through Dunston, thus enabling a bridge over the Tyne to be closed: a further benefit of this diversion was that it passed close to the massive new Gateshead Metro Centre shopping complex, and a station serving the site was opened in the summer of 1986.

In recent years, new 'Pacer' Class 143 DMUs have replaced the older Class 101 DMUs on the N&C, which certainly has a secure future. After several years of operation as a self-contained route, late 1988 saw the introduction of a daily Newcastle-Stranraer Harbour train, worked by Super Sprinters, and this has heralded the start of a new Anglo-Scottish cross-country service, from Newcastle to Carlisle, thence to Glasgow and Southwest Scotland via the Dumfries-Kilmarnock line.

The Settle & Carlisle – Trans-Pennine Controversy?

Of all the trans-Pennine main lines, the Settle & Carlisle railway has long had the most meagre passenger service, as the table below demonstrates. Ironically, in view of recent developments, the current service is probably the best enjoyed by the line in nearly two decades.

Below:
Henschel 0-4-0ST *Thomas Edmondson* stands at Alston station on 17 July 1988 with a South Tynedale Railway train.
David Eatwell

Northbound Passenger Services Over the Settle & Carlisle Line

1957	1972
09.15 London St Pancras-Edinburgh (The 'Waverley')	09.05 London St Pancras-Glasgow (The 'Thames-Clyde Express')
10.15 London St Pancras-Glasgow (The 'Thames-Clyde Express')	09.26 Leeds-Glasgow
10.35 Leeds-Glasgow	21.00 London Euston-Leeds-Edinburgh (Inc Sleeping Cars)
21.00 London St Pancras-Edinburgh (Inc Sleeping Cars)	
Additional Stopping Trains: 5	Additional Stopping Trains: No Service

1981	1988
07.15 Nottingham-Glasgow	08.25 Leeds-Carlisle
10.31 Nottingham-Glasgow	10.45 Leeds-Carlisle
16.05 Nottingham-Glasgow	13.03 Leeds-Carlisle
	16.33 Leeds-Carlisle
Additional Stopping Trains: No Service	Additional Stopping Trains: 1

In the early 1960s, the Settle & Carlisle line enjoyed a reputation as a route over which steam power (some of it unusual) could still produce good performances over the long gradients. 'Jubilee' and 'Royal Scot' 4-6-0s provided staple express motive power — the former were still in use over the line as late as 1967 — while the ubiquitous 'Black 5' 4-6-0s handled stopping services. In 1960, however, a batch of Gresley 'A3' 4-6-2s was allocated to Neville Hill depot in Leeds specifically for Settle & Carlisle services, putting in some memorable performances. Visits by the streamlined 'A4' Pacifics were much rarer, although 60011 Empire of India brought the up 'Waverley' into Leeds on 2 March 1962; however, in the summer of 1963, the Neville Hill 'A3s' were augmented by three 'A1' 4-6-2s, providing a real Indian summer for steam traction over the Pennine fells. It seemed entirely appropriate that BR's official withdrawal of steam traction in August 1968 covered a return journey over the Settle & Carlisle.

Despite all this, the Settle & Carlisle always seemed to have an uneasy existence, and there were many who believed that diversion of Leeds-Carlisle services via Clapham Junction, Ingleton, Low Gill and the WCML was a practical step – indeed, in the early 1960s, BR announced plans to re-equip the whole of this section with colour-light signals, even though passenger services between Clapham and Low Gill had been withdrawn in 1954. During the big freeze of the 1962/1963 winter, the Settle & Carlisle was blocked for several weeks, and all trains were diverted via the Ingleton route.

Closure of the Stainmore line had little effect on the Settle & Carlisle line's fortunes, but the withdrawal of passenger services over the 24 miles between Blackburn and Hellifield had much greater significance, since it robbed the route of feeder traffic from South Lancashire. Intimations of worse things came in the 1963 Beeching Report which advocated closure of all intermediate stations between Hellifield and Carlisle, thus robbing the isolated villages of any decent public transport. However, the incoming Labour government of 1964 announced a reprieve for these services.

In March 1967, BR put forward its revised Re-Shaping Plan, this time advocating total closure of the Settle &

Carlisle line to passenger traffic – the central section, from Appleby to Horton-in-Ribblesdale, would close entirely, the surviving sections being retained for freight traffic. By the summer of that year, however, yet another lifeline was thrown, with a BR announcement that the Settle & Carlisle would not close until the planned Preston-Carlisle resignalling scheme, scheduled for 1970-71, had been implemented; in the event of the Crewe-Carlisle electrification scheme being approved, the Settle & Carlisle line would be singled and used extensively for diversions until the scheme was completed.

With approval for electrification and resignalling in 1970, the Settle & Carlisle line seemed destined to see out its centenary in 1976, although 1970 also saw the final withdrawal of all local services, on 4 May, as well as closure of the Skipton-Colne line, the latter robbing the Settle & Carlisle of a decent East Lancashire feeder service. By now, the whole route between Settle Junction and Carlisle was subject to an overall 60mph speed limit, in order to squeeze more life out of the track, although the majority of the distinctive MR signalboxes remained open to control the still considerable number of freight trains which used the line, particularly at night.

In retrospect, WCML electrification may have been a missed opportunity to encompass singling of the line and resignalling within the overall scheme. Nonetheless the double-track route continued to carry heavy freight traffic, especially as removal of catch-points over Shap meant that unfitted or partially-fitted freights were barred from the WCML.

The fortunes of the line seemed to revive in the summer of 1975, when a Dalesrail service was introduced between Leeds and Appleby on selected weekends, using the still-extant platforms at Horton, Ribblehead, Dent, Garsdale and Kirkby Stephen – this service was sponsored by BR, the National Bus Company, the Yorkshire Dales National Park, and local councils. The following summer, the service was extended to Carlisle, three more stations – Langwathby, Lazonby and Armathwaite – being reopened for this purpose, and in April 1978, a number of trains started from Blackburn serving Clitheroe en route. The centenary of the opening of the line to passenger traffic, on 1 May 1976, was commemorated by the running of special trains and a centenary banquet in Settle, although this tended to overshadow the fact that May 1976 saw the withdrawal of the 'Thames-Clyde Express'; from then onwards, all services would commence from, or terminate at, Nottingham or Leicester.

The next year, 1977, saw the opening of the route to steam excursions – the first indication of a long-term role – and the following years have seen a wide variety of preserved motive power and rolling stock used. The Settle & Carlisle's vital role as a diversionary route continued, although, with a national decline in freight traffic and the phasing out of non-braked goods stock, the number of freight workings declined; one result of this was the closure of several signalboxes.

In May 1982 came the news that all East Midlands-Scotland trains were being diverted via the Hope Valley, Manchester and the WCML, leaving a residual weekdays-only service of two trains between Leeds and Carlisle; the financial implications of sectorisation meant that the surviving through freight traffic would be diverted to other routes. Closure was again in sight, and a well-organised support group – the Friends of the Settle & Carlisle Line – was set up to fight any forthcoming proposals, which were finally issued in 1984.

As anticipated, there was an immediate upsurge in passenger traffic, with the four-coach trains often being extended to as many as nine or 10 bogies. The BR manager appointed to oversee the closure decided to assume a marketing role instead, and stations throughout the UK displayed posters extolling the beauties of the line. Local services, supported by local councils, were reintroduced by BR in July 1986 and the Transport Minister, visiting the line to review the operation, was forced to stand on a packed train! It looked as though a reprieve was on the cards, perhaps underpinned by support from the private sector.

The announcement on 16 May 1988 that the Minister was 'minded' to close the line unless it was sold privately by November 1988 came as a blow to all who had battled to retain the Settle & Carlisle as part of the national network; the magazine *Modern Railways* made the appropriate comment that it would become 'not so much a railway, more a theme park in long drag'. Thus 1988 might have been the last year of the Settle & Carlisle as part of the national network. On 11 April 1989, however, came the surprising announcement, from the Secretary of State for Transport, that the S&C would, after all, remain open as part of the national network.

Below:
Advertisement for proposed sale of Settle & Carlisle line, *The Times*, 14 July 1988.

Following the line's reprieve, a one-day conference on the route's future was held in Leeds in July 1989, attended by BR, local authorities, pressure groups and other interested parties. The main points resulting from the meeting were:
– BR's commitment to spend 'several million pounds' on the line's infrastructure
– vigorous marketing of the S&C
– 'Super Sprinters', faster and more frequent trains, and an all-year Sunday service to be introduced in May 1991
– possible re-introduction of Manchester-Blackburn-Hellifield through services in May 1991.

Morecambe to Leeds – A Trans-Pennine Survivor

In 1960, the future for Leeds-Lancaster-Morecambe services seemed generally secure, with eight trains a day each way between Leeds/Bradford and Lancaster/Morecambe, some of which contained a Carnforth portion detached at Wennington; additionally, there were a number of separate workings between Leeds and Carnforth. All of this was underpinned by heavy freight traffic between the West Riding, the Furness district and Heysham Harbour. The east end of the route carried heavy commuter traffic between Skipton and Leeds, down the Aire Valley, while in the west, the Lancaster-Morecambe/Heysham section was operated by 6.6kV ac electric multiple-units.

Motive power, too, was distinctly 'mainline', with BR Standard 4-6-0s and 2-6-0s on the Leeds-Morecambe passenger workings, and freights handled by Stanier 2-8-0s, 'Jubilees', and Ivatt Class 4 2-6-0s. In the spring of 1962, this variety was augmented by the arrival at Lancaster Green Ayre shed of several 'Patriot' 4-6-0s, which were generally used on passenger services. Diesel power was already interloping, however, in the form of what became the Class 45s, and these generally handled the six/seven-coach trains until the service was turned over to DMU operation in January 1966.

The same month marked the closure of the picturesque section down the Lune Valley between Wennington, Lancaster and Morecambe, as proposed in the 1963 Beeching Report, although the Doctor's other recommendation – withdrawal of the stopping service between Leeds and Morecambe – was not implemented. Nonetheless, this marked the start of an uncertain period for the route, not helped by the diversion of the Sunday service via Skipton, Colne, Blackburn, Preston and the WCML in January 1963, and which lasted for a number of years. As with the Settle & Carlisle, the 1967 Castle Plan went even further than the original plan, recommending total closure of the Settle Junction-Wennington-Carnforth line and permanent diversion of the Leeds-Morecambe service via Colne and Blackburn. Curiously, that decision was reversed late the following year, when BR proposed closure of the Skipton-Colne section of the East Lancashire line. That service was withdrawn in February 1970, and the Morecambe-Leeds service, now reprieved via its original route, settled down to an uneventful existence marked only by the introduction of steam excursions in the mid-1970s and a decline in freight traffic to around two workings a day between Settle Junction and Carnforth. Singling of this section was contemplated, but never carried out.

In recent years, the level of through services has remained largely constant, as the table below shows, but the virtual doubling of the Aire Valley commuter service reflects joint funding by the West Yorkshire Passenger Transport Executive and BR.

Service Levels: Leeds to Morecambe			
	Through Trains	Average Journey Time	Local Trains
1971	8 Weekday (inc 3 to Heysham Harbour) 2 Summer Saturday	2hr 2min	20 (Leeds/Bradford to Keighley/Skipton)
1980	8 Weekday 1 Summer Saturday	2hr 3min	37 (Leeds/Bradford to Keighley/Skipton)
1988	7 Weekday No Summer Saturday	2hr 16min (Additional journey time represents Lancaster reversal)	37 (Leeds/Bradford to Keighley/Skipton)

Motive power over the Morecambe-Leeds line has gone through a number of changes since the early 1980s. Since 1966, Class 101 Metro-Cammell DMUs had formed the mainstay of the service, but the May 1982 changes on the Settle & Carlisle route were accompanied by the introduction of limited-stop trains on the Morecambe-Leeds route, in an attempt to encourage West Riding-Scotland passengers to travel via Lancaster. These services were worked by Class 123 'InterCity' DMUs, recently transferred from the Western Region, which ran nonstop over the 37½ miles between Skipton and Carnforth. By 1984, there was a further improvement, with the introduction of locomotive-hauled stock (usually headed by a Class 31) on these trains, which now originated at Hull and terminated at Lancaster. More recently, however, the service has been turned over to Class 144 Pacer DMUs, perhaps not the most comfortable motive power for a 70-mile journey, and, at the time of writing, the service is once more being worked by 'classic' DMUs.

Now marketed as the 'Pennines Line', and supported by a well-produced colour brochure, the Morecambe-Leeds route seems free from any short-term closure prospect, though there is little chance of its services being developed beyond the present level. However, should BR plan further developments over the Copy Pit line (discussed more fully in the next section) then the future for the Skipton-Carnforth service could look very bleak indeed.

The East Lancashire Line – A Route for Development

Entering the 1960s, the rail network in East Lancashire was still extensive – Burnley passengers, for example, had a choice of two routes to Manchester (via Bury or Bolton), while a Colne traveller could reach Leeds, with one change at Skipton, in around 1¼hr.

Following extensive dieselisation, the London Midland Region introduced, in March 1961, an intensive DMU service between Colne/Todmorden, Preston and Blackpool; a stopping DMU service between Accrington and Preston; and further workings between Skipton, Colne and Manchester. This resulted in a half-hourly service between Colne and Accrington for most of the day. Steam still

predominated on freight services and on some of the summer-dated trains which ran to Blackpool from the West Riding via Copy Pit, although even here diesels were making inroads; the summer of 1962 saw a large increase in the number of what were to become Class 31s reaching the seaside town, and in September 1962, an English Electric Type 3 was noted on these workings for the first time.

As stated previously, the Blackburn-Hellifield line lost its passenger services in 1962, and it was also rumoured that the Copy Pit line, with its sparse regular passenger service (although an important freight artery), was facing complete closure because of land movement affecting the track; no intermediate stations remained open on this section, the last one – Burnley (Manchester Road) – having closed the previous year.

The 1963 Beeching Report recommended total closure for the Copy Pit line and modifications to other East Lancashire services, although the Preston-Colne-Skipton line was to remain open for its whole length. In 1964, implementation began, with a diversion of most Manchester-Colne-Skipton services away from the steeply-graded Bury-Accrington line and on to the Bolton-Blackburn route; by 1966, the Ramsbottom-Accrington section was closed, being cut back completely to Bury by 1972. In 1987, however, the East Lancashire Railway, a preservation organisation, reopened the Bury-Ramsbottom line, and a further reopening to Rawtenstall is planned.

In November 1965, the Rose Grove-Todmorden service was withdrawn, although the daily Leeds-Blackpool train used this route until 1976, when it became a summer-only working. The rest of the East Lancashire network, however, remained intact and, with Leeds-Carnforth-Morecambe trains running on Sundays via Colne and Blackburn, it was proposed that this should be the permanent route for the service, allowing total closure between Settle Junction and Carnforth; the journey time would have been longer, but a much greater population would have been served.

However, not only was this proposal not pursued but by late 1968, the 11¼-mile section between Skipton and Colne was being put up for closure. Little opposition was aroused, and the line closed in February 1970, leaving Colne at the end of a 30-mile-long branch from Preston. One of the links in a trans-Pennine chain had been cut.

In the early 1970s, the Bolton-Blackburn line was singled for much of its length, with a passing loop remaining at Darwen, but of greater interest was BR's decision to include the Rose Grove-Hebden Bridge line (the Copy Pit route) as part of the Preston resignalling scheme, completed in 1973.

Despite the limited passenger service, in the early 1970s there was considerable freight traffic using the route between Healey Mills yard (Wakefield) and the Lancashire towns, and BR clearly thought the resignalling investment to be worthwhile. However, the recession of the late 1970s, coupled with BR's decision to reroute the Healey Mills-Blackburn coal traffic away from the line, meant that by 1982 only one train daily – an Immingham to Preston oil working – was using the Copy Pit line. In 1983, this too was rerouted, and the line closed completely during the winter months. Total abandonment seemed no more than a formality, and resignalling appeared to have been an expensive investment.

Strangely, the impetus for the restoration of Lancashire-Yorkshire services via the East Lancashire route came from a building society! In 1982, the Burnley Building Society merged with the Bradford-based Provincial Building Society, forming the National & Provincial. This required staff to travel frequently between the two offices, and a deal was struck between BR and the building society over the financing of a daily Preston-Hebden Bridge-Bradford train, leaving Preston at 07.18 and returning from Bradford late in the afternoon. The train was open to members of the public, and first ran on 14 May 1984.

From 1 October 1984, BR expanded the service to five trains daily between Preston and Leeds, with one running to and from Blackpool North. By May 1988, this had further expanded to eight trains daily each way, four of which started and finished at Blackpool and York. The provision of new Class 150 Sprinter DMUs shows the importance BR attaches to this service – a far cry from the near-abandonment of the early 1980s. This importance was underlined when, in February 1986, engineers reported geological damage in the 200yd Holme Tunnel and immediately closed the line, buses being substituted between Rose Grove and Todmorden. Fears that the reinvigorated route would be permanently closed proved groundless as BR began a repair programme, which was not completed until late autumn 1986; as a result, Burnley (Manchester Road) was reopened on 29 September that year without any trains – surely a unique happening!

The Pennine Heartland – A Growth Market

A revamp of the Central trans-Pennine services in 1960 was the idea of the North Eastern Region. With the main line services still being handled by 'Jubilee' and 'Royal Scot' 4-6-0s, the North Eastern Region believed that there existed a great potential for new traffic over the Pennines, mainly among business travellers, which could be attracted by an equal-interval service in specially-designed DMUs. While capital costs would be high, operating costs would be much lower than the steam trains they replaced.

The North Eastern Region planners therefore concentrated on dovetailing Liverpool-Newcastle and Liverpool-Hull services. The first proposal was to route the services over the Calder Valley main line, with its relatively easy gradients, but there were pathing problems because of the heavy coal traffic, resulting in the selection of the Standedge route. The Calder Valley line was, however, to get its own provision of new DMUs.

The North Eastern Region was keen to reduce the Manchester-Leeds timing to 1hr, but this would have required six-car DMUs with each car powered, together with considerable capital expenditure to ease speed restrictions. With no prospect then of the future of M62, a 70min Leeds-Manchester timing, inclusive of two stops, was considered commercially acceptable. Based on this decision, the North Eastern Region and its co-partner in the service, the London Midland Region, opted for four power cars per six-car set, with a maximum speed of 70mph. Orders were then placed with Swindon Works for 34 power cars and 17 trailers, with a total of 1,840hp for each six-car unit, the first of which entered service in September 1960.

At the same time, a decision was taken to retain locomotive-hauled stock on Newcastle-Liverpool workings, in order to provide operating flexibility. Between Leeds, Manchester and Liverpool the North Eastern Region was keen that the expresses should conform to InterCity schedule pattern, and interweave with the Hull-Liverpool DMUs to create a precise hourly interval service between Leeds and Manchester. As a result, the NER ordered BR/Sulzer 2,500hp Type 4 diesels (later Class 46), but had to start the new service with 2,000hp English Electric Type 4s (later Class 40), a low-powered locomotive for hauling 10 coaches across the Pennines. Newcastle-Liverpool services were now increased from three to four each way daily.

The introduction of the new service via Standedge marked the end of the Calder Valley as a trans-Pennine express route, since the former Liverpool-Newcastle (via Hebden Bridge) services now terminated at York. As from 1 January 1961, the Calder Valley restaurant car locomotive-hauled services were replaced by Birmingham RCW DMUs (later Class 110); with 720hp/three-car set available, some speed-up of this service was permitted. The basic Calder Valley service was now:

Leeds Central-Manchester Victoria-Liverpool Exchange
Harrogate-Manchester Victoria-Liverpool Exchange
York-Wakefield Kirkgate-Manchester Victoria.

On the Standedge route, the new timetable also came into effect on 1 January. The patronage of the new DMU service initially increased loadings by 40%, with operating costs reduced by 38% – a very creditable performance. While the locomotive-hauled trains retained their traditional restaurant cars, the new DMUs had their own griddle cars, offering meals like steak and chips! To show how tightly timed the new services were, the following table illustrates 1961, 1979, and 1988 Huddersfield-Manchester timings:

Huddersfield to Manchester Schedules (25.8 Miles)

Motive Power	1961		1979		1988	
	Class 124 DMU	Class 40	Class 124 DMU	Class 45/47	Class 150 DMU	Class 47
Time (min)	36½	43	39	40	38	39
Intermediate Stops	1	1	0	1	1	1

The 1963 Beeching Plan proposed the retention of both the central trans-Pennine routes, though with the closure of most intermediate stations, between Manchester and Mirfield on the Standedge route. However, these closures were not carried out until October 1968, by which time Park, Stalybridge, Mossley, Greenfield and Marsden had been reprieved. Despite Beeching, BR kept the issue of duplicate trans-Pennine routes under review, and in 1964 proposed the re-routeing of the Hull-Leeds-Liverpool 'Trans-Pennine' DMUs away from Standedge and on to the Calder Valley, and to provide increased freight paths via Huddersfield. 'Beeching II' in 1965, however, singled out the Calder Valley line for development as the northern trans-Pennine freight artery, carrying traffic from the massive new Healey Mills marshalling yard, and the proposal was shelved.

The year 1967 brought the first indications that some trans-Pennine rationalisation might be on the cards, with BR suggesting that the York-Normanton-Sowerby Bridge-Manchester service might be withdrawn; it was believed that revenue from these services did not even cover direct

Left:
**Sprinter No 150202 pauses at
Stalybridge with the 13.52
Scarborough-Liverpool Lime
Street on 14 June 1988.**
John Glover

costs. Additionally, traffic on the 'core' route via Standedge was beginning to decline, partly because there had been no acceleration in journey time since the start of the decade, but also because there were frequent substitutions of high-density units for the Trans-Pennine DMUs (on which the much-praised griddle cars had now been downgraded to miniature buffets). By mid-1968, closure notices were posted for the York-Normanton-Manchester through service, which was finally withdrawn in January 1970; little track mileage, however, was closed to passenger traffic, and only two stations – Horbury and Brighouse for Rastrick — lost their passenger services.

The completion of the trans-Pennine M62 motorway in 1973 eventually forced BR to re-think its trans-Pennine strategy. For many years, motorists had been forced to use the old Pennine passes with their steep gradients and sharp bends, and which were often blocked by snow; now they had an all-weather, high-speed motorway, allowing fast drivers to travel between Manchester and Leeds in around an hour.

BR's response was some time in coming. Apart from the remodelling of Heaton Lodge Junction in 1970, which permitted slightly higher speeds for Standedge trains between Huddersfield and Thornhill LNW Junction, no significant time improvement schemes had been carried out, and by 1975 passengers were offered the choice of a Manchester-Leeds journey either in an ageing DMU (now with no refreshment facilities) or in Mk 1 stock hauled by a Class 46 or under-powered Class 40. Research highlighted a poor public image and concern about the quality of trains; at the same time it also identified a growth potential, particularly between Leeds and Manchester.

The May 1979 timetable saw a complete recast of services over the Standedge route, designed to meet the motorway competition; Class 47s and more modern Mk 2 stock were drafted on to the service, with some train sets even consisting of air-conditioned coaches — all trains had buffet cars. The 'core' service was hourly between Liverpool and York, with five workings a day extended to and from Newcastle, and the Manchester-Leeds time was cut to 66min, BR still being committed to achieving a 60min transit at some future stage.

Early in the 1980s, there were further developments on the Standedge service when certain Liverpool-York trains started from Llandudno and terminated at Scarborough, thus extending the range of journeys without need to change and also replacing life-expired DMUs with more modern locomotive-hauled stock.

The most recent revamp of central trans-Pennine service took place in May 1987, when, thanks to the allocation of 17 new Class 150/2 Sprinter DMUs, BR's Provincial Sector was able to make further changes. On the long-distance front, the Liverpool-Newcastle service remained locomotive-hauled, though with a reduced number of coaches per train (seven instead of the previous eight or nine), using a dedicated fleet of Class 47/4s to replace the Class 45/1s which had worked most trains since the early 1980s: the coaches were finished in Provincial Services' trans-Pennine livery.

The Llandudno-Scarborough locomotive-hauled service was, however, replaced by a Sprinter service between Scarborough and Liverpool every 2hr, alternating with the Newcastle trains to provide an hourly frequency between York and Liverpool. The introduction of an hourly Sprinter-based Hull-Chester service provided a half-hourly service over the Leeds-Manchester section, covered in exactly 60min inclusive of Huddersfield and Stalybridge stops. However, there have been complaints of serious overcrowding on the four-car formations over this section, and there is a further danger that, when the present Liverpool-Newcastle service is turned over to the 23-metre Express Sprinter stock in May 1990, the public may regard it as a downgrading.

The Calder Valley line has also recently received more modern stock, after soldiering on for many years with the original 1961-built Class 110 DMUs; the majority of services are now worked by Class 150 or 155 Sprinters. Frequency is also good, with 29 trains daily each way between Bradford Interchange and Hebden Bridge, 19 of which are to or from Manchester Victoria; since most run to or from York or Scarborough, the through York-Manchester service via the Calder Valley, discontinued since 1970, has now been restored, albeit using only half of the original route.

The Southern Crossing –
Great Central Closure, Midland Renaissance

At the start of the 1960s, few could have forecast how Manchester-Sheffield traffic would be handled 20 years on. On the one hand was the former Great Central route via Woodhead, electrified only a few years previously and carrying a fast InterCity-type service as well as heavy freight traffic; and on the other, the Midland line, busy as far as Chinley, but beyond which a relatively sparse steam-hauled stopping service meandered through the rural Hope Valley to Sheffield.

The 1963 Beeching Report seemed to confirm this view. The Woodhead route and all its stations were to remain open as a major traffic artery (although the Huddersfield-Penistone line was to close), but all stopping trains were to be withdrawn from the Hope Valley line, probably as a prelude to total closure of the route to passengers.

Later that year, however, came the first faint hint of change, when BR withdrew the Liverpool portion of the Harwich boat train, the Manchester portion being rerouted into Piccadilly in order to allow the same coaching set to work out and back from Parkeston Quay in one day. (A Stratford Class 37 worked the train throughout, including the stretch through the Woodhead Tunnel.) In 1964, an unofficial report, circulating in the Northwest, suggested that the 17 expresses daily in each direction on the electrified Woodhead line should be transferred to the Hope Valley route instead, thus permitting the Woodhead route to become freight-only; 25,000 tons of coal were moved westwards each day through the tunnel, and with the large Fiddler's Ferry power station on the Mersey due to become operational in 1969, an even larger volume of freight via Woodhead was forecast.

A rather more official proposal, also made in 1964, was the withdrawal, after a short life of 10 years, of the electric multiple-unit service between Manchester Piccadilly, Glossop and Hadfield. This was followed by a BR statement early in 1965 that, following construction of a new curve in Sheffield at Nunnery carriage sidings, all passenger traffic in the city would be handled at Sheffield Midland, leaving Victoria to handle only the Manchester electric passenger service.

Evidence of BR's muddled thinking on the south Pennine routes came with Beeching II in 1965, which recommended retention of the Woodhead line as a trunk route for both freight and passengers, citing the newness of the Woodhead Tunnel and the virtual lack of permanent speed restrictions as evidence in the line's favour. By April 1966, both the Manchester-Hadfield/Glossop and the Penistone-Huddersfield services had been reprieved — Woodhead appeared back in favour once more. Rather less noted was the welcome news, in September 1966, that Edale and Hope stations, on the Midland route, would remain open, on the grounds that rail was the only acceptable form of public transport. (The other stations were reprieved later.)

In January 1967, however, BR proposed withdrawal of the Manchester-Sheffield electric service from 5 June 1967, and its replacement with an 'express' DMU service via the Hope Valley; a bus service would provide the Penistone-Sheffield link. BR's justification for this was based on the so-called National Freight Train Plan, which sought to develop key freight arteries and which saw Woodhead as the principal trans-Pennine route for this purpose. However, BR's figures supporting lack of passenger train paths appeared to include an unusually large number of seasonal freight trains (about 40), when compared with the 60 scheduled freights using the line each way daily.

A vociferous anti-closure campaign saw BR agree to a 1968 trial working of a Manchester-Hadfield EMU through the Woodhead Tunnel to Penistone, there to connect with a Huddersfield-Sheffield DMU. Apparently clearances in the tunnel were insufficient, and the idea was not proceeded with. In the same year, all the 'EM2' (nominally Class 77) Co-Co express locomotives were withdrawn, and subsequently sold to the Netherlands Railways. Final appeals against closure proved fruitless, and what was undoubtedly the finest express route between Manchester and Sheffield lost its through services on 4 January 1970, the Huddersfield-Penistone service being extended to Sheffield Midland (reversing via the Nunnery spur) on the same day; at the western end, the Manchester-Glossop/Hadfield commuter service continued to operate.

During the early 1970s, the line fulfilled its role as a dedicated freight route, air-braked and multiple-fitted Class 76s hauling long merry-go-round (MGR) and Speedlink services through the Pennines. By 1977, however, with the recession beginning to bite, the Woodhead route, with its non-standard 1,500V dc equipment and its relative lack of interconnection with other lines, came under scrutiny; despite appeals for its retention and development as a passenger artery, the route closed in July 1981 and has now been lifted completely between Hadfield and Penistone.

The Manchester-Glossop/Hadfield service was soon converted to 25kV ac operation, giving it a secure future, but the recent history of the Huddersfield-Penistone-Sheffield link has been much more complicated, with both West Yorkshire PTE (supporting the Huddersfield-Denby Dale section) and South Yorkshire PTE (supporting Penistone-Sheffield) threatening to withdraw funding at various times. The future of the southern end of the route was secured in May 1984 when the service was re-routed between Penistone and Sheffield via the now-singled Barnsley line, thus bringing the workings totally within the South Yorkshire PTE area; by November 1984, a new station at Silkstone Common had been opened on this stretch. West Yorkshire PTE took longer to convince, but eventually agreed to continue support. The route's future is now secure, although singling of the remaining double-track section had been completed by mid-1989; however, the closed station at Berry Brow is due to reopen in 1992.

Woodhead's decline was accompanied by the gradual renaissance of the Hope Valley line. The first upgrading came on 1 April 1968, when BR diverted the St Pancras-Derby-Manchester service from its highly scenic Ambergate-Chinley line, running instead via Chesterfield and the Hope Valley. From January 1970, with the closure of Woodhead to passengers, the Hope Valley saw a new 'express' DMU service, running nonstop between Sheffield and Manchester in 60min (although the electric expresses over Woodhead did the same trip in 55min with three intermediate stops).

Throughout the 1970s, the services over the route showed a decline, both in overall numbers and journey times, as the table below shows:

	1971	1980	1988
Sheffield-Manchester DMUs	12	17	27
Locomotive-hauled ex-London/E. Midlands	9	1	—
Sheffield-Manchester Fastest Journey Time (min)	60	61	52

By the mid-1970s, the St Pancras-Manchester service had virtually disappeared, leaving the Harwich-Manchester boat train as the only regular locomotive-hauled working through the Hope Valley. The mixture of ageing Derby and Metro-Cammell DMUs working Sheffield-Manchester services was increasingly becoming the subject of public complaint, and with the revamping of Manchester-Leeds services in May 1979 the Class 124 'Trans-Pennine' DMUs were transferred to Hope Valley services, being pooled with the similar Class 123 'InterCity' DMUs recently transferred from the Western Region. At the same time, many services were extended to and from Hull and Cleethorpes, giving a modest service improvement.

The Eastern Region, however, saw the Southern Pennine route as being a candidate for locomotive-hauled services, with Mk 2 stock, and this was introduced in May 1984, using Class 31 haulage. Since, by this time, the Nottingham-Glasgow services had been diverted from the Settle-Carlisle route to use the Hope Valley, the standard of passenger comfort over the southern trans-Pennine artery was considerably increased, with a number of trains using air-conditioned stock and with many services having refreshment facilities. The opening of the Hazel Grove Chord meant that most trains could now be extended from Manchester to Liverpool.

The 1988 timetable recast saw the Hope Valley as part of the central section of a new East Anglia-Northwest service, operated by the 23-metre 'Super Sprinter' Class 156 DMUs and providing a 52min express service between Sheffield and Manchester (older DMUs continued with an 'all stations' service, routed via New Mills Central and Romiley). One feature of this new service was the routing of a number of trains via the Dore South-Dore West curve, thus avoiding a Sheffield call. Again, however, most of these services are operated by two-car units, with the usual complaints of overcrowding — indeed the 1986 10-coach 'European' boat train (from Harwich) has become the two-car 'Loreley' DMU in 1988! It remains to be seen whether this level of comfort remains acceptable in the long term.

Overall, the Hope Valley is now an integral and developed part of BR's national network — a far cry from the Beeching era and threatened closure. This upbeat note of newer trains and more services, serving a wide variety of towns and cities on both sides of the mountain chain, is an appropriate point to end this survey of trans-Pennine rail services.

Below:
The 16.14 Sundays-only Manchester to Lowestoft is seen leaving Disley Tunnel on Sunday 12 June 1988. *Alan H. Bryant*

Bibliography

This present work is not an exhaustive study of any one line, but the historical sections of some of the earlier chapters involved a certain amount of detailed research, and it was felt that local historians would welcome some mention of source material. The following notes are intended as a general guide, and do not represent the sum total of all source material.

Chapter One

Acts consulted included the Newcastle & Carlisle Acts of 1829 (incorp.), 1846, 1849 and 1850, while other primary sources included N&CR half-year reports for March 1850 to March 1853, together with various NER, LNER and BR timetables. Recent articles on the Newcastle & Carlisle line or the Alston branch include: Mike Fenton, 'South Tynedale Railway', *Railway Magazine*, December 1974; P. W. B. Semmens, 'North Eastern Freight', *Railway Magazine*, October 1984 and Michael J. Denholm, 'Newcastle & Carlisle 150', *Railway Magazine*, March 1985.

Chapter Two

The main Act consulted for Chapter Two was the North Western Railway Act of 1846, and useful opening details came from *The Illustrated London News* and *The Railway Times*. Half-yearly directors' reports were again a mine of information, particularly that presented to the share-holders at a meeting held at Skipton on 22 February 1849. The directors' and engineers' reports for February 1850 were also of special interest in terms of constructional details. Other primary sources for this chapter included both BR and LMS working timetables, while John Tolson's detailed article 'Midland to Morecambe No More' in *The Railway Magazine* for April and May 1966 is to be recommended. More recent articles include: M. J. Borrowdale, 'Heysham's Last Boat Train', *Railway Magazine*, July 1975; Martin Bairstow, 'Leeds-Morecambe in Focus', *Railway Magazine*, June 1983 and Stanley C. Jenkins, 'Across the Pennines', *Railway Modeller*, July 1983. *North of Leeds* by Peter Baughan, and *Crewe to Carlisle* by Brian Reed can also be strongly recommended (not only for the light that they shed on the Morecambe to Leeds line but also as models of how good railway histories should be written).

Chapter Three

The Settle & Carlisle line has attracted more than its fair share of attention in recent years, but the best history of the line is still Peter Baughan's *North of Leeds*. Sources for the present study included the Settle & Carlisle Act 1866 (29 & 30 Vic. cap 223), Midland Railway directors' reports (especially that for February 1866) and contemporary journals such as *The Railway Times* and the *Sheffield & Rotherham Independent*. Of the numerous articles churned out in recent years, the best are probably: David Jenkinson, 'The Long Drag in Reality', *Railway Modeller*, January/February 1966; David Jenkinson, 'Modelling Midland Buildings', *Railway Modeller*, November 1963; David Jenkinson, 'Garsdale Road', *Railway Modeller*, April/May 1970; Peter Baughan, 'Centenary of the Long Drag', *Railway Magazine*, May 1976; E. G. Barnes, 'Disaster at Hawes Junction', *Railway Magazine*, February 1971; John Clarke, 'Outpost of the Midland', *Railway Magazine*, March 1966; John Newstead, 'Aisgill: A Suitable Case for Closure', *Railway Magazine*, May 1983; O. S. Nock, 'Settle & Carlisle: Midland Days', *Railway Magazine*, April 1976; O. S. Nock, 'Settle & Carlisle into the New Age', *Railway Magazine*, May 1976; W. Hubert Foster, 'Ais Gill', *Railway Magazine*, June 1976; Jeremy North, 'The Long Drag', *Meccano Magazine*, June 1963 and Andrew R. Wilson, 'Hellifield — A MR Junction', *Railway Magazine*, May 1986.

Chapter Four

Acts consulted for Chapter Four included the Cockermouth Keswick & Penrith Act 1861 and the Eden Valley Act 1858. Other primary sources were *The Railway Times* edition of 7 September 1861 which contained a detailed report of the first CKP general meeting, and an earlier edition of 3 November 1860 that outlined the aims of the CKP promoters. Brian Reed's *Crewe to Carlisle* contains useful background information, while David R. Webb's two-part article 'Between the Solway & Sellafield' (*Railway Magazine*, September/October 1964) describes the background to railways in northwest Cumbria. Professor Pollard's 'North West Coast Railway Politics' (*Transactions of the Cumberland & Westmorland Antiquarian & Archaeological Society*, New Series Vol 52, 1952) also provides much useful data.

Chapter Five

The East Lancashire lines have not received much attention from historians, but there is a wealth of material available for serious researchers. Acts used for this section were: The Blackburn & Preston Act 1844; The Manchester Bury & Rawtenstall Act 1844; The Blackburn Burnley Accrington & Colne Extension Act 1845; The Blackburn Clitheroe & North Western Junction Act 1846 and The East Lancashire Railway Act 1846. Details of the passage of these Acts from the first petitions for leave to bring Bills through the granting of Royal Assent were obtained from *The Journal of the House of Commons* (which journal was also consulted for other chapters). The subsequent history of these lines was culled from a variety of sources including *The Railway Times*, *The Railway Chronicle*, *Bradshaws Shareholders Manuals* and local papers such as *The Blackburn Standard*.

Chapter Six

General background to the railways of the Pennine heartlands can be found in articles such as Peter Baughan's 'Railways of the Spen Valley' (*Railway Magazine* March/April 1964) and Rex Christiansen's 'Pennine Anniversaries' (*Railway Magazine*, July 1977).

Chapter Seven

The Great Central is another somewhat neglected company in relation to railway history, but fortunately George Dow's three-volume *Great Central* provides a worthy memorial to this now-decimated system. Useful articles include: P. W. Semmens, 'Passengers Via Woodhead', *Railway Magazine*, February 1981; Neil Hammond, 'Eight Months Over Woodhead', *Railway Magazine*, February 1981; Peter Hogarth, 'Last Rights on the Woodhead Route', *Railway Magazine*, March 1970 and C. J. Allen, 'Great Central Train Services of 1905', *Railway World*, March 1965. The Midland trans-Pennine route is touched upon in *The Midland Railway* by C. Hamilton Ellis and in a variety of articles such as: John Swift, 'New Mills to Buxworth', *Railway Modeller*, August 1973; John Swift, 'Chinley', *Railway Modeller*. *Railways in the Peak District* by Christopher P. Nicholson and Peter Barnes provides a useful survey of both the Great Central and Midland trans-Pennine routes.

Below:
With pantographs almost at their maximum height, Class 76s Nos 76023 and 76010 make a photostop at Penistone, on the Tinsley-Dinting leg of an enthusiasts' special, on 7 October 1978. Penistone had solid main buildings and extensive canopies, fending off the worst of the Pennine weather. *Les Nixon*